W9-AUR-222

"Let's Drink to Us, Natalie,"

Grant said in a low voice. "To you and me and what the future holds for us."

A tremor shivered through her. "But I don't . . ."

"There you go again," he said with a sigh. "Get this into your head: I'm not trying to hustle you into anything you don't want."

But that, she thought forlornly, was the whole point. What *did* she want from Grant? Her emotions were in a state of crazy confusion. Reason and logic could come up with no convincing argument why she should go on denying herself the fulfillment he offered.

Smiling tremulously, she raised her wineglass to her lips. "Here's to you, Grant."

"To *us!*" he insisted, and smiled deep into her eyes.

NANCY JOHN
is an unashamed romantic, deeply in love with her husband of over thirty years. She lives in Sussex, England, where long walks through the countryside provide the inspiration for the novels that have brought her a worldwide following.

Dear Reader,

Silhouette Special Editions are an exciting new line of contemporary romances from Silhouette Books. Special Editions are written specifically for our readers who want a story with heightened romantic tension.

Special Editions have all the elements you've enjoyed in Silhouette Romances and *more*. These stories concentrate on romance in a longer, more realistic and sophisticated way, and they feature greater sensual detail.

I hope you enjoy this book and all the wonderful romances from Silhouette. We welcome any suggestions or comments and invite you to write to us at the address below.

Karen Solem
Editor-in-Chief
Silhouette Books
P.O. Box 769
New York, N. Y. 10019

NANCY JOHN
Never Too Late

Silhouette Special Edition
Published by Silhouette Books New York
America's Publisher of Contemporary Romance

SILHOUETTE BOOKS, a Division of Simon & Schuster, Inc.
1230 Avenue of the Americas, New York, N.Y. 10020

Copyright © 1983 by Nancy John

Distributed by Pocket Books

All rights reserved, including the right to reproduce
this book or portions thereof in any form whatsoever.
For information address Silhouette Books, 1230
Avenue of the Americas, New York, N.Y. 10020

ISBN: 0-671-53606-0

First Silhouette Books printing July, 1983

10 9 8 7 6 5 4 3 2 1

All of the characters in this book are fictitious. Any resem-
blance to actual persons, living or dead, is purely coincidental.

Map by Ray Lundgren

SILHOUETTE, SILHOUETTE SPECIAL EDITION and
colophon are registered trademarks of Simon & Schuster, Inc.

America's Publisher of Contemporary Romance

Printed in the U.S.A.

Other Silhouette Books by Nancy John

Tormenting Flame
The Spanish House
To Trust Tomorrow
Outback Summer
A Man for Always
So Many Tomorrows
Web of Passion
Make-Believe Bride
Summer Rhapsody

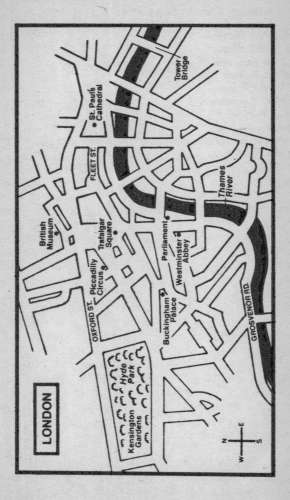

LONDON

Tower Bridge

St. Paul's Cathedral

FLEET ST.

Thames River

British Museum

Trafalgar Square

Piccadilly Circus

OXFORD ST.

Parliament

Westminster Abbey

Buckingham Palace

GROSVENOR RD.

Hyde Park

Kensington Gardens

N
W E
S

Chapter One

"A man is a man is a man," Natalie Kent quipped to herself in an effort to stifle her nervous qualms. The fact that Grant Kilmartin happened to be a wealthy, thrustful tycoon, running his own highly successful property-development company, was neither here nor there. She had to regard him as simply another potential client.

Uncomforted by this philosophizing, she gave herself a critical checkover in the small mirror of the elevator that was whisking her to the twelfth floor of a modern office block near Trafalgar Square. She prodded back a few stray tendrils of the lustrous chestnut hair that framed her oval-shaped face in soft, loose waves, ran a licked finger along each of her delicately curved brows and hoped that she hadn't overdone the green shadow which accentuated her wide golden-brown eyes.

On this bright April morning Natalie had somewhat changed her usual business-hours image of neat, quiet efficiency, which was designed to impress the well-to-do women who chiefly employed her services. Beneath her swinging black-and-white-check coat she wore a cowl-necked dress in supersoft orange wool, which didn't cling provocatively but did full justice to her slender, shapely figure. High-heeled slingbacks, a twisted gilt necklace and a subtle hint of expensive French perfume added the finishing touches. Beside her black patent shoulder bag she was carrying a portfolio of sketches and photographs which she had carefully assembled last night.

All this surely should have added up to a feeling of brimming professional confidence, rather than the reverse. There was positively no reason, she firmly instructed her quailing inner self, to be so darned jittery about meeting this particular man.

The elevator halted and the doors slid back. Gathering herself together, Natalie stepped out to the lobby and walked to the reception desk, which was manned by an attractive, rather plump woman in her early thirties.

"How can I help you?" she inquired pleasantly.

"I'm Natalie Kent. I have an appointment with Mr. Kilmartin. I phoned yesterday."

"Oh, yes, Mrs. Kent." The woman smiled and buzzed through to announce Natalie's arrival. Replacing the phone, she gestured to a row of low-slung red leather chairs beside a trough of potted greenery, standard decor for the smart office, Natalie noted. Okay, but hardly inspired. "Mr. Kilmartin's secretary says that he's tied up at the moment. He won't keep you waiting long."

"Thanks."

The minutes ticked by, and in between handling the switchboard, the receptionist passed a few friendly comments about the weather and a royal charity performance that had been televised over the weekend. Suddenly Natalie found herself blurting out, "What's he like . . . Mr. Kilmartin?"

She received a conspiratorial grin. "For heaven's sake, don't tell my husband I said so—he'd kill me—but GK is the dishiest man you've ever seen."

Natalie felt annoyed with herself for having given the wrong impression. "I meant," she said a trifle stiffly, "what's he like to do business with?"

"Oh, that! Well . . . he's straightforward enough, but very tough. He knows exactly what he wants, and he makes sure he gets it. I'd advise you to . . ." But Natalie wasn't to learn the receptionist's good advice. Instead, she was given a swift warning glance as an inner door behind the desk was pulled open.

The first sight of Grant Kilmartin gave Natalie the strangest sort of feeling. Her heart seemed to judder, and the breath stuck fast in her throat. It wasn't that he was particularly handsome, but never before had she encountered a man with such an aura of virile masculinity, of such sensual dynamism. He was a good six-foot-two or -three and powerfully built, seeming to fill the doorway through which he had just emerged. His face was leanly angular, with prominent cheekbones and a deep forehead crowned by a mass of crisp hair that was a rich dark brown with coppery glints. He was casually jacketless, wearing navy-blue trousers leather-belted above his lean hips, and a cream shirt teamed with a red-and-gold-striped tie.

Natalie found herself being subjected to a slow all-over appraisal, and his deep-set slate-gray eyes gleamed appreciatively.

"Sorry to have kept you waiting, Mrs. Kent," he drawled, his arrogant smile making it clear that this was only a token apology. "Will you come through now?" The voice was low-pitched, with a resonant timbre that set little quivers darting through her; she detected, too, a faint Scottish lilt to it that matched with his name. As she rose nervously and went forward, he extended a hand in greeting. The grip was firm, decisive, but far from being the matter-of-fact handshake he would have given a male business caller. There was a blatant acknowledgment of her womanhood in the clasp of those long, lean fingers, a lingering pressure that made it impossible for her to draw away until he permitted it.

Natalie felt annoyed at his presumption, and even more annoyed with herself for having found the physical contact exciting.

Grant Kilmartin's office was impressive, as she had guessed it would be, a fitting environment for a business tycoon. Light and spacious, and expensively furnished in tones of beige and brown, it had three large windows that looked down over Trafalgar Square. Yet the room wasn't designed merely for show. It was very much the functional office of a hardworking, practical executive. The large steel-and-leather desk was scattered with correspondence and architect's drawings. Grant Kilmartin was a man in a hurry to make his first million, she reminded herself, thinking of the paragraph she'd read about him in yesterday's financial pages.

He waved Natalie into a chair and himself took a casual perch on the edge of the desk, his long legs stretched out before him, his fingers loosely interlinked.

"Well, Mrs. Kent?" he inquired invitingly. "When you made this appointment with my secretary you didn't explain why it was you wanted to see me."

"I want to talk to you about your development project at Princess Dock," she began, cursing herself for sounding nervous.

Grant Kilmartin's straight dark eyebrows lifted. "That project is scarcely off the ground yet. Do you mean that you're interested in purchasing one of the apartments?"

"No way! The sort of prices you'll doubtless be charging would be out of my range. I've come to offer my services as an interior-design consultant."

"I see." The look in his dark eyes changed from warm to cool. "What a pity, then, that I'm not in need of an interior-design consultant."

"You mean that I'm too late?" Natalie asked, bitterly

disappointed. "You've already fixed up with a designer to handle the work?"

"No, I didn't mean that," he clipped. "What you're suggesting, Mrs. Kent, just doesn't come into my scheme of things. In the case of Princess Dock I've negotiated to buy a derelict warehouse building together with the adjoining land and the dock basin. I plan to transform all this into a block of luxury apartments with surrounding gardens and various facilities. But the internal decorative details of the apartments will be left to the purchasers' own choice. If you like," he added in a condescending tone that suggested he'd be putting himself out to do her a great big favor, "I'd be willing to pass on your name to anyone interested. It would then be up to them whether or not they employ your services."

"Thank you, Mr. Kilmartin, but that's not what I had in mind. I'm suggesting that we should work together right from the early stages. I could meet prospective buyers at the moment when they first show interest." His expression was neutral, indicating that she'd at least gotten his attention, and she went on hurriedly, "The general run of people, I've found—even those with plenty of money—feel dismayed at the prospect of making decisions about decorative schemes for their homes. But if a trained expert can meet them and talk to them, and then put forward ideas for imaginative treatments, well, in my experience—"

"Your wide-ranging and lengthy experience?" he cut in, one dark eyebrow hoisted in mild derision.

"I've had enough experience to know what I'm talking about," Natalie snapped back. The nerve of him, she thought indignantly, when he himself couldn't be more than thirty-three years old against her own twenty-seven. "On more than one occasion I've been told that it was my suggested scheme for the interior decor which persuaded a client to buy a particular house or apartment . . . what finally clinched the deal. So you really need someone like me to help you in this venture, Mr. Kilmartin."

"I don't need help from anyone," he contradicted in a biting tone. "Least of all from you. The sort of help you could offer is entirely outside the scope of my project."

"In that case," Natalie retorted acidly, "I suggest that your project should be revised. If you weren't determined to wear blinkers, you'd be able to see that my services would be invaluable to you."

"Blinkers?" The slate-gray eyes turned granite-hard. "So, in your considered opinion, Mrs. Kent, I don't know my own business. Is that what you're saying?"

Natalie flushed a deep pink, shocked at where her quick tongue had landed her. No matter how justified her retort had been, she could do without a reputation for rudeness in her professional dealings.

"I'm sorry, I shouldn't have let fly like that," she murmured, with every appearance of meekness. "But I came here with a perfectly reasonable proposition. I've merely been asking for a chance to demonstrate what I could do for you. Obviously, though, you just don't want to know, so I won't waste any more of your valuable time. Or my own!" She stood up and turned toward the door. "Good morning, Mr. Kilmartin."

"No, hang on!" As Natalie swung around in surprise, he continued with a quirk of his lips, "You intrigue me, Mrs. Kent. Perhaps, after all, I should hear you out . . . give you, as you ask, the chance to demonstrate what you could do for me."

"Do you really mean that?" she asked suspiciously.

"Must I put it in writing?" He treated her to a bewitching smile. "How do you suggest we proceed from here?"

It was only too obvious from Grant Kilmartin's suddenly affable manner and the way he let his gaze roam slowly over her slender body that he was superbly confident of his ability to dazzle a woman with his charm. Natalie knew the type. She could deal with this man as easily as she'd dealt with others who'd tried their luck. Nevertheless, there was something about him that unnerved her; she sensed that he could be a threat to her emotional stability. She needed to crush the cowardly impulse to turn tail and flee.

"What I'd like to do," she explained, snatching a shaky breath and getting a grip on herself, "is to take a preliminary look at the building."

"Feel free," he invited, with a careless shrug of his broad shoulders. "Whenever you like."

"But won't it be locked up?"

"Naturally."

"I'll need to see around inside," Natalie informed him. "And also I'd want to study the architect's plans to give me an idea of the general treatment."

He looked amused by her persistence. "You're not asking much, are you, Natalie?" With a swift glance at his wristwatch, he went on smoothly, "We'll discuss the matter over lunch."

Natalie stared at him, stunned. She saw the glint of challenge in his slate-gray eyes, and shivers of apprehension flurried through her. There was only one sensible reaction to what was obviously going on in Grant Kilmartin's brain—to slap him down hard. On the other hand, if she played along with his suggestion, pretending to take it at face value, there was just a chance that she might be able to win him over to her point of view. The possibility of a lucrative contract was worth taking a few risks for, wasn't it?

"Thank you," she said demurely. "That sounds like a nice idea."

"Glad you think so," he murmured in a voice as soft as silk. "I'll just slip next door to have a word with my secretary, and then we'll get going." When he returned a few moments later he was carrying a long cardboard tube with some rolled-up papers inside. "Ready then, Natalie," he said cheerfully, shrugging into his jacket, which had been draped across the back of a chair.

Natalie didn't care for the easy way he'd taken to using her first name. Neither did she like the disturbingly possessive way he took her arm—cupping her elbow with those long fingers—as he escorted her to the elevator. Grant Kilmartin was altogether too sure of himself; he needed taking down a peg or two. But with caution, an inner voice warned. She must firmly keep in mind the aim and object of accepting this invitation to lunch with him.

Thinking he would walk her to a nearby restaurant, Natalie was surprised when they emerged from the elevator into the basement car park. His car was a dark blue Alfa Romeo—low-slung and powerful. As they zoomed up the ramp and out to the street, she inquired, "Where is it we're going?"

"You'll like the place," he said confidently. "Just your style, unless I'm greatly mistaken about you—which I doubt," he added, flashing her a quick smile that seemed to jolt through her like an electric shock. "Mrs. Natalie Kent," he mused. "There is, I take it, a *Mr.* Kent?"

"He's in New Zealand," she replied shortly.

"How very careless of him," Grant commented.

"Careless?"

"To leave his beautiful wife all alone and lonely in London."

"What makes you think that I'm either alone or lonely?" she flipped back.

"Wishful thinking on my part?" he suggested with a grin. "Tell me about yourself, Natalie, and this imprudent husband of yours."

She ran the tip of her tongue around dry lips, then

said unwillingly, "As a matter of fact, we're divorced, and he's married again."

"So you're fancy free?"

"A better way of putting it," she stated flatly, "is that I'm uninvolved. And I have every intention of staying that way."

Grant threw back his head and laughed. "A woman with your fantastic looks, Natalie, doesn't stand a snowball's chance in hell of remaining uninvolved."

"Isn't that up to me?"

He shot her another sideways glance. "You must be very strong-willed, then."

"I am," she said emphatically.

"But not, I venture to suggest, ice-cold. That's just an act you put on."

Natalie edged farther away from him in her seat, too disturbingly aware of this man's vibrant sensuality. The warmth that seemed to emanate from his body and the subtle tangy scent of his skin was making her feel quite dizzy. Watching his lean, suntanned fingers splayed around the gearshift, she was dismayed to find herself imagining those same fingertips trailing an erotic path across her flesh. She gave an involuntary little shiver, and stared rigidly ahead through the windshield. Grant chuckled softly, and she had a mortifying suspicion that he could guess the sort of thoughts that were passing through her mind.

Leaving the Strand, Grant headed along Fleet Street and skirted the massive splendor of St. Paul's Cathedral. When he had driven farther eastward for a few more minutes, Natalie suddenly realized where they must be making for. "Are you taking me to see Princess Dock?"

"Eventually. First, there's the little matter of the lunch I promised you."

Quite soon they reached a Thames-side dockland

area, with tall warehouse buildings looming all around them. Grant finally pulled up by an ancient inn positioned right alongside the river. It must have been built three or four centuries ago, Natalie gauged. The red brick walls, clad with creeper, leaned at crazy angles and its windows had diamond-leaded panes, sparkling now in the bright spring sunshine. Small wrought-iron tables were set out in the cobbled forecourt, and more tables could be seen on a trellised upper balcony. A swinging sign that proclaimed the inn's name, the Hangman's Noose, depicted a man's lifeless body dangling from a gibbet.

"How gruesome!" Natalie commented.

"In the old days they used to hang rebellious sailors near here," Grant explained. "At a spot called Execution Dock."

Natalie glanced around her and asked, "Which of the warehouses is the one you're going to develop?"

"You can't see it from here. But when we get to our table on the balcony, which my secretary will have booked, we shall be looking right at it."

Inside, the Hangman's Noose was just as attractive. Everything, as far as Natalie could judge, was genuinely ancient, from the low black-beamed ceiling to the well-worn tables and chairs of solid English oak and elm. The barroom was pleasantly full without being overcrowded.

"This place is fascinating," she said enthusiastically, sipping the soda she'd asked for. "It will be a big asset to your new development, having such a quaint pub almost on the doorstep."

Grant nodded. "One of many assets. I've never felt so sure of a project as this one."

"The Kilmartin Development Corporation is a fairly new company, isn't it?" she asked probingly. "I don't think I've come across the name before."

"I've been operating on my own for about eighteen

months now," he explained. "At the moment I'm just completing a shopping arcade at Maida Vale, and there's a leisure center in one of the new towns under way."

"Before you set up on your own, were you with one of the big development corporations?"

Grant's answer was a curt nod, and she watched a shadow flicker across his face. Finishing his tankard of beer in one swallow, he said briskly, "Let's go upstairs and eat now."

It looked as if she had touched a raw nerve, Natalie mused as she followed him up the narrow enclosed stairway. They were shown to a corner table on the balcony from which they had a superb view across the River Thames with its bustling traffic. A tug hauling a string of laden timber barges exchanged hooted greetings with a sightseeing boat that was packed with tourists. Over by the far bank, a fast-moving police launch cut smoothly through the water, leaving a creamy wake. On their own bank the view was less pleasant: they overlooked a sprawling area of dereliction. All around the dock basin—a stretch of dirty water covered with slimy weed and sodden driftwood— lay the evidence of demolished buildings. Arising out of this sea of rubble was the gaunt framework of a large Victorian warehouse with its broken windows roughly boarded up.

Yet Natalie could see this unlovely scene quite differently. As always when viewing a prospective designing job, it was as if she possessed a pair of magic lenses which transformed what she was looking at. Thus, the ramshackle building now before her suddenly gleamed with steam-cleaned stonework and brilliant new white paint. Balconies embellished each story, and a fine new entrance portico bestowed an added grandeur. She visualized green lawns and landscaped gardens sweeping to the dock basin, whose murky waters would have been filtered to sparkling clarity and adapted into a private marina, while mature trees and shrubs would have been planted to lend grace to the scene.

Whoever had first recognized Princess Dock as ripe for residential development had a real imaginative flair, seeing ahead from its present state of forlorn neglect to a new and vital future, she thought appreciatively.

"It's beautiful," she breathed. "Fantastic."

"It's a terrible mess," Grant commented wryly.

She turned to look at him, her golden-brown eyes shining. "But it has such fabulous possibilities. Oh, how I'd love to live in one of those apartments myself." She sighed, adding wistfully, "If only I was that sort of filthy rich."

From Grant's surprised expression it seemed that he was viewing her with a new sort of respect. "You really can size up the possibilities, can't you, Natalie? Most people have no ability to appreciate the potential of a development project. They regard a building like that derelict warehouse as fit only for demolition, and they need to be shown an artistic impression of how the site will look when it's finished before they can be convinced otherwise."

Natalie seized on his words triumphantly. "Isn't that exactly what I've been saying regarding the *interior* treatment? Okay, some people—a few people—seem to possess the ability to achieve a pleasant effect in their homes. But for the majority, just give them the bare shell of an apartment—however luxurious its potential —and they're at a loss to know what to do with it. And why should they be expected to know?" she demanded with rhetorical emphasis. "In all kinds of other situations, like legal problems, accounting matters and so on, people expect to employ a trained expert to advise them."

Grant quirked a dark eyebrow. "And you claim to be a trained expert in interior design?"

"I'm entitled. I did a three-year college course, then worked as an assistant to a leading West End design consultant before setting up on my own a couple of years ago."

"So much experience crammed into your young life," he mocked.

"I'm twenty-seven," Natalie retorted angrily. "Did *you* regard yourself as young and inexperienced when you were that age?"

"Far from it," he admitted, his dark eyes dancing with amusement at her flash of spirit. "But what I really meant was, how did you manage to fit all this activity in, plus getting married and divorced? You haven't been idle, that's for sure."

Natalie shrugged. "I married early, while I was still at college. Then . . . then I was forced to quit studying, but I went back to college again after we split up."

"Did your husband object to his wife being a student?" Grant inquired.

"No, it wasn't that." Her lovely eyes clouded a moment, but she forced herself to remain calm. After all these years she had to learn to speak about this traumatic period of her life matter-of-factly, not keep shying away from the remembered pain. Looking up, she met Grant's gaze and said in an even tone, "Actually, I had to give up my studies because I became pregnant."

"Oh, I see, you have a child. Boy or girl?"

Natalie clenched her fingers under the table. "My baby was born dead."

"That's tough," Grant said sympathetically, then asked, "Was that the cause of your marriage breaking up?"

"You could say it was what brought things to the boil."

Grant's forehead knotted in a frown. "A hell of a moment for a man to walk out on his wife."

"Correction, it was the other way around. I walked out on my husband."

The waitress came up for their order, but Natalie's mind was only half on the menu in her hand. Grant's questions had jolted her back to the painful episode of her marriage. She had been just coming up to her nineteenth birthday when her mother and father, returning home from a vacation in Sicily, had lost their lives in an airplane crash. A few weeks later, while she was still in shock from this grievous blow, she met Dudley Kent at the wedding of a mutual friend. They had chatted together all through the reception and Dudley asked her to have dinner with him that evening. Natalie had found it immensely flattering that a handsome, mature man of thirty should take such a keen interest in her.

In the days that followed it had been only too fatally easy to get starry-eyed about him. She saw Dudley as her knight in shining armor, making her small world secure once more. They were married after a whirlwind courtship, spent their honeymoon in Spain, and on their return set up a home in Dudley's apartment in St. John's Wood, close to the famous Lord's Cricket Ground.

Her happiness had been short-lived, though. Far from being a chivalrous knight, Dudley turned out to be a carping and critical husband. No longer was her youthful lack of sophistication hailed as charming, but condemned as gauche stupidity when she found it beyond her to act the smooth, poised hostess at the frequent dinner parties he insisted on giving for his business contacts.

After eighteen months of marriage, toward the end of her second year at college, Natalie discovered she was pregnant. Even though she had planned to complete her studies before starting a family, she was overjoyed. It seemed to her that a child might be exactly what their marriage needed to give it a fresh chance. Despite Dudley's unconcealed irritation when she broke the news to him, she clung to the hope that as soon as he saw the beautiful baby she had produced, his heart would melt with love and tenderness.

Alas, things didn't work out that way.

Dudley owned an import-export agency, involving a lot of complex wheeling and dealing which Natalie never fully grasped. Sometimes, with growing frequency, this necessitated his being out late in the evening or took him away from home overnight. Left on her own, she tried to bolster her sagging spirits by knitting for the baby, doing needlepoint pictures, and copious reading. But she couldn't prevent herself from brooding. She was painfully aware that her marriage needed a miracle to hold it together. She and her husband were just too diametrically opposed. The final crunch had come when Dudley was away one weekend, attending an exporters' conference at Harrogate Spa. On the Saturday afternoon Natalie experienced some alarming internal pains, and called the doctor. She was admitted to the hospital in premature labor, and a message was sent for her husband to come at once. But there was no record of Dudley checking in for the conference. It seemed he had never even registered.

Her mind racked with worry and misery, Natalie had given birth to a stillborn son in the early hours of Sunday morning. Dudley finally turned up at the hospital late that evening, having been directed there by neighbors when he'd arrived home. There was a sullen wariness in his eyes as he stood beside the bed looking down at her.

"Well, this is a fine mess," he began.

"Where were you, Dudley?" she demanded, unable to keep accusation from her voice.

"What do you mean . . . where was I?"

"Don't pretend. You were sent for, and it turned out

that you'd never intended going to Harrogate. I suppose . . ." Natalie gulped, suddenly understanding what she'd been so naively blind to before. "I suppose you were with another woman."

Dudley glared at her, angry at being caught out, then shrugged defiantly. "It's no big deal, Natalie. What do you expect? You've hardly been much fun for a man these past few months."

Tears filled her eyes. If her husband had looked ashamed, penitent, she might have been prepared to forgive him. Instead, Dudley was at his most cold and bitter, finding yet another excuse to put her down. "You are a healthy young woman and your pregnancy was perfectly normal. All the tests showed that. I never expected you to lose the child."

In that instant Natalie knew that there could be no future for them together. During the following days of convalescence, her opinion never wavered. Whatever life might hold for her, she had to be free of this man. Luckily, Dudley didn't try very hard to change her mind, and the divorce went through without a hitch.

Natalie had refused to ask Dudley for alimony. Mercifully, she had the proceeds of her father's life insurance to fall back on, and she used this to complete her college course in design and furnishing, which she'd dropped after becoming pregnant. Graduating with distinction, she had secured a job with one of the best-known designers in Mayfair, starting at the bottom and working her way up. Then just over two years ago, on her twenty-fifth birthday, she took the plunge and set up in business on her own.

To Natalie it was a bold, momentous step. To the rest of the world it was a non-event. No one beat a track to her door to demand her brilliant services. She had to go out and pitch for customers, taking on all kinds of tiny jobs that scarcely paid the rent. But she kept going somehow, putting everything she had into each commission she undertook, until she eventually began to win. Satisfied clients passed the word that Natalie Kent could be relied on for a highly imaginative job without charging the earth. One day she had a request from the owner of a smart florist's shop in Knightsbridge to update her premises, and the result caught the eye of a well-known actress. The new decor designed by Natalie Kent for the star's Belgravia apartment was prominently featured in a popular monthly magazine, and since then she'd really made headway.

All the same, Natalie knew that it would be fatal to sit back and rest on her laurels. She was constantly on the lookout for challenging new assignments that would further upgrade her reputation. The day before, a short paragraph in the financial columns had mentioned that the Kilmartin Development Corporation was planning to convert a derelict warehouse in London's dockland into a block of super-luxury apartments. Natalie had promptly called and made an appointment to see the managing director, deciding that she had nothing to lose by going straight to the top. And now here she was, having lunch with the boss man himself, Grant Kilmartin.

"Is this a new diet craze—all fish?" he inquired wryly as the waitress departed with their orders.

Natalie glanced at him across the table. "Sorry?"

"You ordered smoked mackerel for starters, with grilled rainbow trout for the main course. Want to change your mind?"

Coloring, she tried to pass it off with a joke. "No, thanks. Fish is reputed to be good for the brain."

Grant grinned amicably. "You were miles away, weren't you, Natalie? Not very flattering to me." He looked questioningly into her eyes. "What were you so deep in thought about?"

"Ideas for the decorative treatment of Princess Dock," she lied. "What else?"

"How tiresomely single-minded you are." He sighed, then raised his wineglass in salute. "Here's to you . . . the most intriguing and exciting woman I've encountered in a long while."

Natalie's smooth brow creased in a frown. "I wish you wouldn't say things like that."

"You don't care to be described as intriguing and exciting? That's a very unfeminine reaction."

"We're supposed to be here for a business discussion," she pointed out coolly.

"You may be," he countered, "but I'm not. My reasons for asking you to have lunch with me were quite different. I want to get to know all about you, Natalie Kent. By the way, I like the dress you're wearing. The color is exactly right for that lovely chestnut hair of yours. Very attractive, very seductive."

Natalie flushed violently, remembering the care with which she'd selected her outfit this morning. Suitable for impressing a man, she'd calculated. But it seemed that she'd overdone it. She wished now that she had worn something severer and presented a brisk, competent image when she'd walked into Grant Kilmartin's office. But if she hadn't dressed this way, her interview would probably have lasted just a few brief minutes and she wouldn't now be lunching with him. At least this way, she consoled herself, she still had a slender chance of persuading him to give her the interior-design commission she was seeking.

"How did you get to be in the construction business?" she asked, aiming to divert the conversation into safer channels.

"I guess it's in the blood. My father was a civil engineer."

"Was that in Scotland?"

He shook his head, smiling. "As it happens, I've

never lived there. The slight Scots accent is what I picked up from my parents."

"You've lived in England all your life, then?"

"Far from it. I was born in Kenya, but that was merely by chance. It was where my father happened to be working at the time I arrived. He was a consultant for a firm that built bridges and viaducts in all parts of the world. He was always on the move, and my mother and I trailed around with him. So my upbringing was thoroughly international."

"It must have been interesting," Natalie commented.

"Sure, I had a great childhood. It wasn't so much fun for my mother, though, never having the chance to get a proper home together and put down roots."

"I can imagine." Natalie paused, then added artfully, "That's a problem *your* wife doesn't have to contend with."

The glint of amusement in Grant's eyes showed that he knew she was dangling the bait. "If I *had* a wife," he agreed levelly. "Which I haven't."

Natalie flushed at having been rumbled. Nevertheless she felt ridiculously pleased to discover that he wasn't married. Not that it affected her one way or the other, of course, since she didn't intend to get involved with this man. There was no denying, though, that it made her feel vitally alive to be in Grant's company. Other men had paid her compliments. Other men had looked at her with admiration, with unconcealed desire. But never before had she known this exhilarating feeling of being rated as extra-special in a man's estimation.

"Your father and mother—where are they living now?" she blurted, in an effort to hide her discomfiture.

"They're both dead, unfortunately." Grant gave her a quick smile. "So you see, I have no one but myself to consider. Now, tell me about *you*, Natalie. Have you parents living? Brothers and sisters?"

She shook her head. "No, I was an only child too, and both my parents were killed in a plane crash some years ago."

Grant met her eyes in a look of sympathy. "What age were you then?"

"Eighteen—just coming up to nineteen."

"And at college, I assume?"

"Yes."

"It's no wonder, then," he said slowly, "that you plunged into the wrong marriage. You can hardly be held to blame for making a bad choice. What was your husband like?"

Natalie stiffened. "I'd prefer not to discuss my marriage."

"Okay, we'll call the subject off limits until I know you better." He reached out and touched her hand where it rested on the table, stroking the soft skin with his thumb. "So we're a couple of poor little orphans, Natalie. A good reason, don't you think, for us getting together?"

"A feeble one, if you ask me," she stammered, pulling her hand free. She felt dismayed at the way his touch had sent tremors of excitement running through her like wildfire.

Grant grinned at her, unabashed. "Then I'll think up some better reasons. Let's see . . . when's your birthday?"

"May. May seventeenth."

His dark eyes widened. "Really! How extraordinary."

Natalie couldn't help giggling. "You're not going to try telling me that your birthday is May seventeenth too?"

"Would you buy it, if I did?"

"Not a chance."

"Then I won't waste my breath. But it *is* true that I'm a bull."

"I beg your pardon?"

"Taurus, the bull," he explained patiently. "Our sun sign."

"Oh, yes, of course."

A smile touched his lips. "What's the omen, d'you think, for the clash of two Taurus personalities?"

"I see no reason," she countered, "why we should clash at all, Mr. Kilmartin."

He sighed. "We will if you stick to calling me that. The name is Grant. To continue, Natalie, what sort of music are you into? Pop? Classics?"

"More classics than pop. I bought a Stephen Sondheim album the other day which I adore."

"Andrew Lloyd Webber?"

"Oh, yes, I love him too."

"Then I'll get two seats for the new show of his that's just opened."

Natalie descended to earth with a bruising bump. "Oh no you won't!"

"You've seen it already?" he asked disappointedly.

"No, I haven't, but . . ."

"Some other man is taking you?"

"Not that either." The thought that it might have been wise to *pretend* that she was being taken by another man crossed her mind much too late. Giving Grant a straight look, she added explicitly, "I'm not going to the theater with you because . . . well, I don't happen to want to."

His eyes held hers captive. "You can't mean it, Natalie."

"I do mean it. Very definitely."

This time he injected a note of wistfulness into his sigh. "How can such a lovely woman possess such a

cruel streak in her nature? You can't imagine the
pleasure you'd give me. And it would boost my ego no
end to be seen as your escort."

"The last thing your ego needs is a boost," she
flashed. "It's already dangerously overinflated."

Despite herself, Natalie was enjoying this lunch.
How pleasant it would be, she thought longingly, to be
swept along by Grant Kilmartin into a lighthearted
affair. She was terribly tempted—but it was far too
risky. Instinct warned her that she could never hope to
emerge unscathed from any kind of romantic involvement with him.

Natalie stared down at the red-and-white-check ta-
blecloth, tearing her eyes away from the dark, seductive gaze that seemed to melt her bones. She found
herself looking at Grant's hand again, the long fingers
now curled around the stem of his wineglass. Tiny
bronze-colored hairs grew at his wrist where it was
circled by the wide gold band of his watch. She could
visualize the firm-contoured, muscular forearm that
stretched up under his shirtsleeve, out of her vision.

"At least tell me this, Natalie," he said softly. "Is
there a special man in your life just now?"

He'd given her another way out. All she needed to
do was to meet his gaze and say that there was such a
man. Instead, she weakly shook her head and glanced
away across the dereliction of Princess Dock. "You . . .
you said you were going to take me to look over the
warehouse," she reminded him. "Hadn't we better get
going?"

Grant nodded, and signaled for the check. "First off,
we have to pick up the keys from the watchman's
cottage down the road."

The high corrugated-iron gates around the site were
heavily chained and padlocked. Grant selected a key
from the bunch and let them into the rubble-strewn
enclosure beyond, which extended right to the dock

basin. Tucked under his arm was the long cardboard tube containing rolled-up drawings, which he'd collected from his car. When they came to a granite bollard with a convenient flat top, he spread these out for Natalie to see.

"This first one is an impression of what the finished development will look like," he told her. "I think the artist has done a good job."

As Natalie studied the color-wash drawing, she exclaimed in astonishment at how everything so precisely fitted in with what she'd visualized from the pub.

"Which proves that you and I are very much on the same wavelength." Grant smiled. "The first moment I set eyes on Princess Dock, I saw its possibilities."

Natalie began to feel a lot more optimistic about her chances of winning a commission from him. Smiling back, she said, "We certainly do appear to be thinking along the same lines."

He paused. "I hope you mean that, Natalie," he murmured softly, his eyes warm and intimate.

She glanced away, annoyed. Would the wretched man never skip the chance to flirt with her? Taking a breath, she ventured in a level tone, "Perhaps you can now see the sense of my suggestion that we should pool our expertise and work together."

"Not so fast, Natalie. Before I agree to anything, you're going to have to win me round to the right mood."

Her cheeks flamed with anger. He had a colossal nerve, hinting that he expected sexual favors as a *quid pro quo* for any business he might put her way. She was tempted to give him a scathing retort, but she kept a curb on her tongue. She wasn't about to throw away a big chance like this just because Grant Kilmartin fancied her and wrongly imagined that she could be coaxed into bed.

"Can we look around inside now?" she asked coolly.

"Sure." He rerolled the drawings and slid them back into the tube. "I warn you, though, it's dirty in there. You must take care not to mess up that fabulous outfit you're wearing."

Besides being dirty, it was dim and dark inside with all the windows boarded up, just a few splinters of sunlight striking through the crevices here and there. Grant explained that the ground floor would be given over to an entrance foyer, communal lounges and restaurant, administrative offices, squash and badminton courts, plus a heated indoor swimming pool and a solarium. Together they began to mount the bare-boarded staircase, pausing at each floor for Grant to indicate how it would be divided into apartments. Already, even in such unfavorable circumstances, Natalie felt a bubbling excitement as creative ideas jostled for space in her brain.

Finally, when she was feeling slightly breathless from climbing so many stairs, they reached the top and emerged onto the flat roof. The panoramic view was fantastic. Eastward was the ever-widening River Thames with its complex layout of docks; westward was the graceful outline of Tower Bridge and, adjoining it, the solid four-square structure of the Tower of London, home of the colorful Beefeaters and the setting for so much of Britain's history. Beyond that were distant glimpses of other famous old London landmarks amid the modern high-rise buildings.

"What a marvelous place this would be to have a penthouse!" Natalie exclaimed.

"That's what I thought, too. It could be made into something really special . . . very spacious, with its own private elevator, and an extensive roof garden."

"You mean, you've already got plans for a penthouse?" she queried. "It wasn't shown on that drawing."

"True." Grant patted the cardboard tube. "I've got a separate drawing right here."

"May I see?"

"Of course." Again he pulled out the plans and spread one of them open for her to see. It was the architect's technical drawing, which Natalie's training had taught her to read. She became deeply absorbed, visualizing a luxurious penthouse apartment in place of the warehouse's rubble-strewn roof. It was almost the same as if she were actually walking around inside the completed structure, able to pick out interesting angles and exciting vistas for decorative treatment.

"It should have a contemporary feel," she murmured to herself rather than to Grant. "Clean, clear colors and modern fabrics, used with restraint. But it needs a few carefully chosen antique pieces to make a definite statement. Those alcoves on either side of the mantel in the living room just cry out for a pair of huge oriental vases . . . something like that. And a washed silk Chinese carpet to coordinate with them. Yes, that would give a splendid effect . . . blue and rose and beige, one of those dragon motifs." She sized up the measurements on the drawings. "Twenty feet by fifteen should be about right."

The breeze from the river caught a tress of her finespun chestnut hair, blowing it across the velvety skin of her brow. As she absently brushed it aside, she became aware of Grant's warm breath fanning her neck.

"Natalie!" he whispered.

She wheeled around in alarmed protest, only to find herself looking into his dark eyes, which were only centimeters from her own. Her legs suddenly shaking, she made a clumsy attempt to step back from him, but Grant's hands came out and gripped her shoulders. The contact, even through the fabric of her coat, was electrifying. She went rigid, the sheet of plans clenched tightly in her nervous fingers.

This was crazy. Hadn't she vowed never to allow any man to get through her defenses again? Yet here she was letting Grant Kilmartin—a womanizer if ever there was one—work his smooth charm on her. How amused he must be, that she was succumbing so readily. She ought to be freezing him off now with a scornful glance and a few crisply pointed words. But all she could do was to stand and look up at him foolishly, as if hypnotized, while her heart thudded with excited anticipation.

Grant's hands moved caressingly over her slender shoulders and down the length of her arms, drawing her closer against his lean, husky frame. Helpless to move, Natalie gasped aloud as his lips touched her left temple and trailed with little nibbling kisses down the silky chestnut waves that lay against her cheek. Then, suddenly, he claimed her mouth and his arms went about her in a breath-robbing embrace. Involuntarily her own hands crept upward to fold around his neck, the tips of her fingers digging into the hair which grew in tiny crisp curls at his nape.

Somewhere out on the river a tugboat hooted, as if in derision. The blaring sound snapped Natalie back to her senses. "Don't," she stammered, thrusting away from him fiercely.

Grant released her, his dark brows knitted in a frown. "For pity's sake, what's the matter?"

"You've no right to . . . to act like this . . . just because I agreed to come up here alone with you."

"Agreed?" he echoed in a mocking tone. "You more or less forced me into this situation."

"That's ridiculous," she protested furiously.

"Consider the facts, my dear Natalie. You can't deny that you've been flashing a green light all along the line.

First, having pleaded for an appointment to see me, you turned up dressed to make any man drool at the mouth and think of the quickest way to get you into bed. When I suggested lunch, you jumped at the invitation, and you can't pretend that you weren't flirting with me across the table. Afterward, you showed great eagerness to look over this place, knowing that we'd be entirely alone up here. How else did you expect me to act?"

"I expected you to act like . . . like a gentleman," she said with all the dignity at her command—which wasn't much.

"Oh, grow up," he snapped impatiently. "We're living in the nineteen-eighties, and we fancy one another, right? So what's against us doing something about it?"

"What makes you imagine that I fancy you, as you put it?"

Grant laughed mirthlessly. "You were in the process of giving a very good demonstration, when all of a sudden you went cold."

"I came to my senses, you mean."

He turned away from her, standing by the stone parapet and staring out across the wide river. When he spoke again, his voice was harsh and uncompromising. "Didn't it go something like this, Natalie? You came to see me today determined to persuade me to pass some lucrative business your way—by hook or by crook. Just now you allowed me a tiny sample of what I could expect in return . . . then you suddenly switched off the heat in a plain hint that I had to promise delivery before I was permitted any more. How's that for an accurate scenario?"

Outraged, she blazed, "It's a foul thing to suggest."

"Then why did you allow me to kiss you just now?" he demanded implacably.

"I . . . I didn't *allow* it. I had no choice."

"Because I overpowered you with my superior strength?" His voice was laden with irony. "In that case, Natalie, how d'you explain that when you'd decided things had gone far enough—for the present—you were able to break away from me without the least difficulty?"

Natalie had no answer to give him, short of admitting the truth—that he had overpowered her, though by his incredibly potent aura of sexuality rather than by his superior physical strength. Held in his arms, she'd felt every nerve in her body responding in a way that far exceeded anything she'd ever felt before—even when she was married. Years ago, an innocent virgin, she had dreamed of this kind of passionate spark between a man and a woman. It was what she had hoped to find with Dudley, but in vain. Stunned by the tragic death of her parents, she had welcomed his kisses and caresses with gratitude, believing that true physical passion would follow in due course. But her marriage had failed to bring the sensual enchantment of her dreams. Then almost at once had come the start of her slow disillusionment that had blighted her feelings about love and sex. Since the breakup of her marriage, not one of her dates had succeeded in stirring her beyond the fleeting pleasure of a good-night kiss.

Until today. Her whole body was still trembling in the aftermath of Grant's kiss. Despite her anger, despite her contempt for him, she felt a shaming urge to close the gap of hostility that separated them now and belatedly offer herself for another kiss . . . a kiss that would inevitably sweep them into a crescendo of feverish lovemaking. Endeavoring to keep her voice steady, she faltered, "There's no point in us standing around here arguing. Clearly, any deal there might have been between us is now off."

"If you say so."

"I do say so. The conditions you impose are unacceptable."

"As far as I can recall," Grant said coldly, "I haven't attempted to impose *any* conditions."

Natalie felt a kind of loathing for the man. He was playing with her, dangling the prospect of a prestigious commission if she succumbed to him sexually. Well, she wasn't going to remain here and be played with. Better abandon all her hopes than to hand victory to Grant Kilmartin. She could imagine only too clearly how it would be if she didn't make her escape from the slippery slope he had laid out for her. His kisses would grow more intimately demanding, while her own resolution to resist him shredded away.

There was only one sensible course open to her—to flee at once, before she was trapped. Already she knew that it would be difficult to forget Grant Kilmartin, to thrust from her mind those magical moments when he had kissed her. But that was the price she would have to pay if she wanted to retain her self-respect.

She walked purposefully to the stairhead jutting above roof level, avoiding the rubble which was strewn everywhere, and said in a firm, clear voice, "I'm leaving."

"So soon? But you haven't even glanced at the plans for the individual apartments."

"There's no point, now."

Grant held her gaze for a seemingly endless moment, then said quietly, "Okay, I'll drive you home."

"Thanks, but I can manage," she retorted.

"I advise you to accept my offer," he said with a twitch of his lips. "You're a long way from a bus stop here, and you'd never find a cruising taxi in this district. So come on."

"Very well," Natalie agreed between clenched teeth. Without exchanging another word, they made their way downstairs, their footsteps clattering on the wooden treads. Outside in the sunshine Grant locked up and returned the keys to the watchman, and still in silence, they walked back to his car.

"Where is it you live?" Grant asked, holding open the passenger door for her.

"I have a studio at Chandler's Wharf," Natalie told him as she reluctantly got in. "That's just off—"

"Camden High Road," he finished for her, and grinned. "I know it intimately. It was one of my development projects."

"One of yours?" Natalie looked at him in puzzlement. "But the conversion there to homes and workshops was done quite a few years ago."

"I handled it for the firm I was with at the time."

"Oh, I see." She found herself adding, in all sincerity, "You made a very good job of it."

"Thank you. I'll be interested to see the place again, now that it's been lived in for a while." He closed the car door and walked around to get in beside her.

They fell silent once more as they headed across London, Grant skillfully dodging the worst traffic jams by threading through side streets. Though the journey took less time than Natalie had dared hope, it was still uncomfortably long. All the while, she was intensely aware of him, of the heat and scent of his maleness. She took care not to look at him directly, but kept finding herself flicking him a covert glance from behind the shelter of her silky lashes. In profile his face had a rough-hewn look that accentuated his forceful masculinity.

At last they turned through the arched entrance to Chandler's Wharf and Grant drew up in one of the parking spaces marked out on the paved courtyard. Natalie felt a sharp sense of disappointment. This was it: their relationship was over and finished before anything had really begun.

For heaven's sake, she chided herself angrily as she slid out of the car, she was letting her emotions get out of control. She'd merely sought a business deal with Grant Kilmartin—a long shot which hadn't materialized. So what? There was no reason whatsoever for her to feel this heavy weight of depression.

Chapter Two

"Well . . . good-bye," said Natalie, reaching for the handle of the car door. "Thanks for driving me home."

"Aren't you going to offer me a cup of tea?" Grant made it a criticism of her inhospitality. "I could do with one after traipsing around that dusty warehouse. Besides, I'll be interested to see what you've made of the studio you occupy."

She hesitated, her mind flailing around for an excuse, but she could hardly refuse such a reasonable request. "Just as you like," she said ungraciously. "My place is number five . . . the one in the corner."

There was always a sense of tranquillity in the courtyard, a high brick wall screening it from the busy road. Rambling one-story buildings lined the other three sides, relics of the days when the Grand Union Canal, which ran close by, had been one of London's busiest transport arteries. Now expertly converted into a series of quaintly pretty residences-cum-workshops, these old wharf buildings offered sanctuary to a number of young professional people who, like Natalie herself, were all connected with the arts in one way or another. The clapboard walls gleamed with fresh white paint, while window boxes and round wooden tubs, planted with tulips and hyacinths, scented the air and added attractive splashes of color.

Natalie's front door opened directly onto the spacious open-plan living room, with her working area on a slightly higher level at one end. Here she had her drawing board and bench, a mini-office unit with desk and filing cabinet, plus stacks of laminated white shelving laden with color charts, fine-art catalogs, design manuals, swatches of fabric and various other samples. As she entered, Grant on her heels, she was greeted by the unexpected sound of a voice from her television set. How had she managed to leave it switched on? Then she spotted the lithe, lean figure of Riccardo Manzini lounging among the billowy cushions of her plum-colored sectional sofa.

"Ciao, Natalie, *cara,"* he called in the softly caressing voice that was habitual to him. "I did not want to miss the big football match from Rome, but my own TV . . ." He shrugged expressively. ". . . it has gone on strike once more." He pressed the remote-control button and the commentator's voice died in mid-sentence.

Natalie sighed inwardly. Riccardo *would* have to choose this particular afternoon to come in while she was out and make free with her home. Normally she wouldn't have minded one bit. It was routine for residents at Chandler's Wharf to leave a spare key with neighbors so they could let in the gas man or whoever. They were a friendly bunch, casual and openhanded, which was the way Natalie liked it. Or had, until this precise moment of time. Then she noticed the frown of annoyance on Grant's face, and another thought struck her. Perhaps, on the contrary, it was a piece of luck that Riccardo was here. Darkly handsome, with a flashing smile and long-lashed melting brown eyes, he was the archetypal dream of a Latin lover. If Grant Kilmartin misinterpreted her relationship with Riccardo, it might put the brakes on his bedward ideas about her.

"This is Riccardo Manzini, who lives next door," she introduced, turning back to Grant. "Riccardo makes the most lovely cameos, which sell like hotcakes.

Riccardo, this is Grant Kilmartin. He's a property developer. We've been looking at a dockland warehouse that he's going to convert into apartments, and he kindly drove me home."

The two men nodded an acknowledgment, Grant coldly polite, Riccardo with his usual outgoing friendliness. "Is Natalie going to design for you, Mr. Kilmartin?" he asked. "She is very talented, you will discover, very artistic, as well as being such a beautiful woman."

Grant didn't speak. Instead he looked at Natalie and left her to answer.

"No way!" she said emphatically. "It was a possibility, but not anymore."

Grant's face was a mask. "Are you in England for long?" he asked Riccardo tersely.

"Who knows? For the moment I am very content here, and I am fortunately able to earn a good living." He glanced at Natalie inquiringly. "I had better leave you now, I think."

"No, don't go, Riccardo," she said hastily. "Mr. Kilmartin has only come in for a cup of tea. Tell you what, be a darling and put the kettle on while I take my coat off. There's a new packet of those oat crunchies you like so much in the larder." Why not lay it on with a trowel? she thought defiantly.

As Riccardo disappeared into the kitchen, Grant met her eyes in a challenging look. "So what was all that about there being no special man in your life, Natalie?"

She gave a vaguely dismissive smile as she slipped off her coat and tossed it onto the avocado velvet bergère chair. "How do you like my treatment of the studio?"

For a moment longer his gaze remained accusingly on her face. Then with a shrug he briefly glanced around. "Very nice, I suppose."

"Such high praise!" she said nonchalantly, but she couldn't help feeling disappointed by his lack of interest in her decorative treatment of the room.

Grant's lips twisted in an expression of scornful amusement. "Were you fishing for flattery, Natalie?"

"Who, *me?*" Oh, darn the man, she'd let him get under her skin. Adopting an uncaringly casual pose, she said lightly, "I'd better go and give Riccardo a hand. Not that he isn't perfectly at home in the kitchen. He's a marvelous cook." True at least as far as *spaghetti alla bolognese* was concerned—Riccardo's one culinary skill.

"Quite the all-rounder, isn't he?" Grant sneered, turning away to study a Salvador Dali print on her wall.

In the kitchen, Natalie found Riccardo dropping teabags into the pot. He rolled his soft brown eyes at her and whispered conspiratorially, "A property tycoon! I am very impressed. You seem to have him nicely caught on your hook."

Natalie gave a high, melodious gurgle, projected for Grant to overhear. To Riccardo she murmured, "You've got it all wrong, it's purely a matter of business. Not even that now."

Riccardo shook his head knowingly. "The way he looks at you, *cara*, it is as if he would like to gobble you up. And at me, he casts daggers."

"That's because he thinks you're . . . well . . ."

"I perfectly comprehend what he thinks about you and me." Riccardo grinned. "What you are *making* him think."

Natalie flushed. "I just want to stop him getting any ideas about me."

"He already has very many ideas about you." Riccardo leaned forward and gave her an affectionate peck on the cheek. "Very well, we shall play your little game. But you realize, I hope, what a risk I am taking for you," he added with a rueful grin. "If Maria were to get the wrong impression, she would be angry as only an Italian girl can be angry."

Natalie laughed, and whispered, "Don't worry, I'll square it with Maria."

When they returned to the living room, Grant was still standing before the Dali painting, as if he hadn't moved a muscle. He refused a cookie, but accepted a cup of tea and took a seat on her hard-backed carved Jacobean chair, an uncompromising expression on his angled face. With a contented sigh Riccardo relaxed beside Natalie on the sofa, draping an arm loosely across her shoulders.

"Do you find that chair comfortable, Mr. Kilmartin?" he inquired with a considerate little smile.

"It will do for the short time I'll be here," Grant muttered. "I'd hate to outstay my welcome."

"But there's no need for . . ." Natalie trailed off, not knowing what to say.

There was an awkward silence while Grant drank down his tea. Setting the cup aside, he rose to his feet and gave Riccardo another cool nod. "Nice meeting you, Mr. Manzini." At the door, he held Natalie's gaze for a long, throbbing moment, then said brusquely, "Good-bye, Natalie. It's been an . . . interesting afternoon."

"Good-bye, Grant," she said with a painful lump in her throat, and closed the door on him.

"I will just wait until he has driven away," said Riccardo from the sofa. "Then I too will go."

Natalie shook herself. "Don't you want to watch the end of the football match?"

"It will be over by now, *cara*. Anyway, it wasn't a very interesting game. The state of play in this room was far more absorbing."

She sighed. "Thanks for giving me a bit of moral support, Riccardo."

"Moral support? Is that what you call it?"

"What would *you* call it?" she countered.

He shrugged eloquently. "The stirring up of a man's jealousy, perhaps?"

"That's crazy! Why should I want to make Grant Kilmartin jealous?"

"Some devious female reason?" He gave her a more serious look. "*Cara,* it is not surprising that the man is very attracted to you. . . . Who in his senses would not be? I would fall in love with you myself, if I were not already in love with Maria."

"How is Maria?" she asked, to ease the subject into a safer channel. "I've not seen her around these last few days."

"She has not been here," Riccardo said sadly. "We only manage to see each other now when I go around to her father's café." He sighed. "Poor Maria, she works far too hard, what with helping there and looking after her young brothers and sisters."

Riccardo's romance had been sadly blighted. Just two days before Maria's people were due to fly to Naples for the wedding, her mother had been rushed to the hospital with a heart attack. The marriage was postponed indefinitely and Maria hurried to London to step into her mother's shoes. Now Signora Gaspari had died and Maria's father needed his daughter's help all the more. The only bright spot was that Riccardo, following her to England, had been able to set up a workshop here and was prospering reasonably well.

Natalie smiled at him sympathetically. "I do hope things work out for you soon. You and Maria deserve to be happy."

"You too, *cara.* But you deliberately throw aside any chance of happiness."

She adopted an air of injured surprise. "Just because I don't happen to fancy one man . . ."

"No," he said reproachfully. "Because always you run away from the idea of falling in love, *cara.*"

"You're such a romantic, Riccardo," she said with a smiling shake of the head.

"Is that a crime?"

"No, not a crime. Just very Italian."

"Perhaps you could benefit from a transfusion of good Italian blood. You need to let yourself fall in love, Natalie . . . you need it very badly."

Love, she scoffed to herself when he'd gone. There was no equating the sort of feelings Grant Kilmartin had aroused in her with love. He had jolted her emotional stability, stirring up an awareness of physical needs she had managed to keep subdued since the time of her marriage. During the intervening years, the men she'd allowed to date her had been no more than amusing escorts with whom she could relax after a hard day's work. They had helped to create the sophisticated image a successful career woman needed, and their admiration had been a boost to her morale. But she'd refused to let these short-lived relationships develop into anything approaching an affair. And afterward, the memory of each man had floated off into a sort of mental limbo in which their names and even their features tended to become intermixed.

But it was going to be different in the case of Grant Kilmartin. With a chilling certainty she knew that he would never be forgotten. Henceforth she'd have to live with the tormenting dream of being held in his arms, pressed close against the length of his rock-hard masculine body. Natalie shivered, and swung around to head for her bedroom, intending to change into jeans and a sweater. Then she stopped abruptly, her eye caught by something that rested on the carved oak chest which served as a room divider just inside her front door. It was the long cardboard tube containing Grant's plans and drawings of the Princess Dock development.

Natalie went over and picked it up, pondering. Why

had Grant brought this inside with him and not left it in his car? And had leaving it here been just an oversight, or had it been quite deliberate, giving him an excuse to return? Surely the latter. She couldn't imagine Grant Kilmartin forgetting something that was of such importance to his business.

So . . . he would be back! The thought sent eddies of excitement swirling through her body, and her breath came more quickly. Then she took herself sternly to task. Grant Kilmartin spelled danger.

With sudden decision she replaced the cardboard tube where Grant had left it. If he dropped by, she'd hand it to him at the front door and firmly say good-bye. If he called, she would tell him to collect it at Riccardo's next door, explaining that she'd be out. Either way, Grant ought to get the message that she didn't want anything more to do with him.

But later that evening, after fixing herself scrambled eggs for supper, then finding she had no appetite . . . after restlessly prowling around the flat unable to settle to anything, she picked up the tube again and slid out its contents. For long minutes she studied the various plans and drawings. What a gem of a job it would be for an interior designer. The sort of people who'd be purchasing the apartments at Princess Dock wouldn't think in terms of economy. They'd want sheer, unadulterated luxury.

Hardly aware of what she was about, Natalie spread out the plan for the penthouse beside her drawing board, using a couple of heavy art catalogs to stop it from curling, and picked up a pencil. Before long several sheets of her pad were covered in a series of squiggly notes and sketches which would make sense to no one but herself. Presently she pinned a sheet of crisp white cartridge paper to the board and fetched brushes and paints. With bold, deft strokes she conveyed a rough but highly effective conception of the penthouse's master bedroom . . . a romantic symphony in tones of blue and gold, with elegantly striped walls and a rich madonna-blue carpet, the huge, ornate brass bedstead having a quilt that was much frilled and beribboned. The open patio doors gave a glimpse of an attractive roof garden, and bright reflections from the river far below were splashed across the molded ceiling.

She was deeply absorbed in a second sketch—the living room this time—when she was startled by a knock at her door. She rose and went over, asking cautiously, "Who's there?"

"It's me, Diane."

Natalie opened up to admit her friend, Diane Fielding, who lived just across the courtyard, occupying a studio apartment with a pretty bow window in which she displayed her delicately etched glassware. Diane possessed a flawless complexion and a mane of raven-black hair, inherited, she liked to point out, from her Spanish grandmother.

"My date just dropped me off home," she explained as she stepped inside, "and I saw that you were still up by the lights on. So I thought I'd look in for a cup of coffee, if there's one going." She raised her dark eyebrows questioningly. "How come you're working so late?"

Natalie shrugged. "I just didn't notice the time."

"Lost in the throes of creation, huh? It's gone two A.M."

"Heavens, I had no idea."

Moving across to look at the drawing board, Diane gave a whistle of admiration. "I say, these are really good. What a fabulous place it must be. Where did you pick up this job, Natalie?"

"Well . . . it isn't exactly a job," she confessed, coloring slightly. "I . . . I'm doing these on spec."

Diane glanced at her, surprised. "That's unusual for you. I thought you only took definite commissions."

Natalie colored more deeply. "In actual fact, there's no hope of my landing a contract as a result of this."

"So, why . . . ?"

"It's more in the nature of an exercise. I happened to have the plans, and I thought I'd amuse myself by dreaming up a decorative treatment."

"Surely *anyone* would fall for a scheme as good as this. You've really surpassed yourself this time, Natalie. Who's the client, by the way—or should I say non-client?"

"Oh . . . just a man."

"No man," Diane observed dryly, "is *just* a man." She spoke as one who regarded herself as an authority on the subject. In the couple of years Natalie had known her, Diane had run through a whole string of men. Each one, while he lasted, was the most wonderful creature alive, but at the end of the brief affair she parted from him without the smallest sign of heartbreak. Neither, unlike Natalie, did she appear to bear any lasting scars from the experience of a failed marriage and divorce. "So who exactly is he?" she repeated. "This man, this client or whatever."

"His name," Natalie replied impatiently, "is Grant Kilmartin. Not that it can mean anything to you."

"Oh, but it does!" Diane looked impressed, intrigued. "Grant Kilmartin . . . well, well, well!"

"You don't mean to say," Natalie demanded, hating the thought, "that he's one of your ex-boyfriends?"

"No such luck. I only know *of* him, really, though I did see him in the flesh once at somebody's party. It was his wife I knew, a very top-drawer, cool, enameled lady."

"His wife?" Natalie echoed, swept by an icy chill.

"She wanted some glassware engraved," Diane explained, "and I went round to their house in Holland Park to see her about it. I happened to notice their wedding picture on a side table, and I thought he looked terrifically dishy." Catching sight of Natalie's face, she added quickly, "Hey, it's okay . . . they're divorced now."

"I see." Natalie made a big effort to get a grip on herself. "I can't imagine why we're discussing Grant Kilmartin," she said tartly. "You dropped in for a cup of coffee, so I'd better go and make it."

Diane followed her and stood leaning in the kitchen doorway. "Why did you say there's no hope of you landing any business from those drawings you're doing?" she asked curiously. "If it's to do with one of Grant Kilmartin's developments, he's got to be interested in anything as good as you've come up with."

"He won't be," Natalie snapped. "You can take my word for it."

Diane's dark brows narrowed shrewdly. "So you've had a row with him. How come?"

"I scarcely even *know* the man," Natalie pointed out, evading a direct answer. "I read in the paper yesterday about a new project of his, so I went along to see him. But Grant Kilmartin made it clear that he didn't require the services of an interior designer. End of story!"

"So why have you been burning the midnight oil making those sketches?"

"I told you, it's just a sort of exercise . . . for my own amusement."

"But you've been provided with a set of architect's plans and drawings."

Natalie lifted her slim shoulders in a dismissive shrug. "Oh, he just left those by mistake, and—"

"He's *been* here?"

Why did Diane have to be so persistent, and so darned logical? "He took me to see the site this afternoon," Natalie explained impatiently. "It's in a very out-of-the-way spot in dockland, and the chances of my getting a taxi were nil, so he offered to drive me home.''

Diane chuckled. "The man bothered to take you to see the site," she declaimed ironically, "even though you insist that there's no hope of his giving you a commission as a result. Then he drove you home and came in with you. And on top of that he left his drawings here, so by a happy 'chance' he'll have to call back for them. End of story nothing! This looks like the start of something big, Natalie. Lucky you."

"Oh, shut up. I told you, I'm not interested in the man." But back in the living room, as they were sipping their coffee, Natalie said casually, "You mentioned that you'd met Grant Kilmartin at a party once, Di. How did you get on with him?"

"I said that I *saw* him. We didn't get around to being introduced, alas. Not that there would have been much point," she added ruefully. "He was very much otherwise engaged with a devastatingly sexy blonde."

"How long ago was that?" Natalie asked, shocked by the fierce stab of jealousy she felt.

"Oh . . . about a year ago, I should think. Maybe more."

"*After* his divorce?"

Diane nodded. "The funny thing was, though, that the woman he was with was very much a lookalike of his wife. When I commented on that to the guy I was with, he said that Grant Kilmartin always seemed to go for the same type of female—cool, Nordic-type blondes. Seems there'd been quite a string of them since his marriage broke up." She glanced speculatively at Natalie and added, "It looks, though, as if he's decided to extend his range a bit now, with you."

Ignoring that pointed remark, Natalie asked, "Why did his marriage break up, do you know?"

"I can guess," Diane said with a laugh. "From what I

saw of Mrs. Melissa Kilmartin, she wasn't the sort to put up with her husband playing around."

Much too abruptly, with a bright smile on her face, Natalie burst out, "Did you have a nice evening, Di? Where did you go?"

"Point taken." Her friend grinned. "We'll change the subject. But first promise me one little thing: if you really don't want the guy yourself, Natalie, you'll point him in my direction and give him a gentle push. Okay?"

Next morning it was wet, a steady downpour of rain spattering the surface of the canal, which Natalie overlooked from her rear window. The work she had neglected yesterday was waiting to be done. At her drawing board she rolled up Grant's plans in readiness for him to collect them. She was about to put her own sketches away out of sight, when a stubborn obstinacy overtook her. There was no denying that her roughly drawn ideas for the penthouse were darned good. So why not let him see them, see what he'd be missing? Maybe there was even a slender chance that he would have second thoughts and offer her a contract on *her* terms, not his.

So she laid the drawings aside, still in full view, and got down to color schemes for the split-level apartment at the Barbican which Lady Aston was currently considering. Undeniably, Celia Aston had proved a very profitable client. Sir Matthew Aston, a wealthy City financier, was insistent that his wife should find a new London home which would properly reflect his elevated position in the world and complement their mansion in Hampshire, but nothing Lady Aston had come up with so far appeared to fill the bill. A spacious Hampstead apartment with fine views across the Heath was too suburban, he'd decided, and the quaint little mews house in Belgravia was poky and inconvenient.

With each new prospect, Natalie was called in to

provide a decorative scheme. The fees she received helped to pay the rent, but it was frustrating to keep producing inspired ideas, none of which ever came to fruition. She also felt a bit embarrassed, as if she were taking the Astons' money without delivering the goods, but Lady Aston assured her that this was nonsense. It was no fault of Natalie's, she'd pointed out, that her husband was such a difficult man to please.

Natalie spent a restless morning and achieved very little. One entire color scheme had to be abandoned when she suddenly remembered that the particular shade of chartreuse green in the velvet pile carpeting she'd visualized as ideal for the Astons' drawing room had been discontinued. How could she have been so stupid? Sighing, she glanced across at the French bracket clock which she'd picked up in a job lot at a country-house sale in the Cotswolds. Time to get herself some lunch. Why hadn't Grant Kilmartin contacted her yet? she wondered edgily. He must have missed the Princess Dock plans by now, even if he'd genuinely forgotten them yesterday.

She didn't hear from him all day, and by the next morning she could bear the suspense no longer. Best to get it over and done with, she decided angrily. Picking up the phone, she punched out the number of the Kilmartin Development Corporation and asked for Mr. Kilmartin's secretary.

"Oh, yes, Mrs. Kent, I'll put you through to Mr. Kilmartin." From her tone of voice, it was almost as if she'd been primed to expect her call. So the whole operation had been a setup, she thought resentfully, from the moment Grant had walked out of her flat leaving the plans behind. And she'd fallen for it! He would undoubtedly take this call as a sign that she was anxious to keep things going with him—even that she was willing to pay his outrageous price for giving her the commission she so dearly wanted.

"Hello, Natalie," he greeted her cheerfully, just as she was about to hang up. "Nice of you to call me. What can I do for you?"

As if he didn't know! Steeling herself against the insidious attraction of just hearing his voice, she said briskly, "About those plans you left at my studio . . . shall I mail them back to you?"

"So that's where I left them. How careless of me."

"Careless?" she queried with heavy sarcasm.

"Call it addle-headed, if you like," he said easily. "Listen, how about me coming round for them this evening?"

"No!" she cried in sudden panic.

"Will you be out?"

If she said yes, Grant would only suggest coming some other time. "Well, not actually," she admitted. "But it won't be convenient."

"You mean that boyfriend of yours will be there?"

"Riccardo isn't my boyfriend." It was out before she could stop herself. Much better to have let Grant keep the idea that she and Riccardo had something going.

"You could have fooled me," he commented in a dry tone. "He seemed thoroughly at home in your flat. He also appeared to have his own key."

"We're next-door neighbors," Natalie reminded him.

"Lucky Riccardo, if that's how you act toward your neighbors. I had no idea, when I was working on the Chandler's Wharf conversion, that it would turn into such a cozy little setup for the residents."

"Let's get back to the point," she said frostily. "I'll mail those plans back to you today. Okay?"

"No, don't do that. I'll drop by this evening earlyish —let's say seven o'clock. You shouldn't have anything heavy going by that time."

Before Natalie could make any comeback, he'd rung

off and she was left seething with fury. But during the course of the day her anger subsided. It was replaced by a firm, cold resolve to impress Grant Kilmartin with her professional ability and disabuse him once and for all of any *un*professional ideas he might be harboring about her.

Natalie had to go out that afternoon, to track down some wall fabrics she wanted for the Chelsea apartment she was designing for a fashion model who was suddenly all the rage. Returning home, she deliberately changed back into her working gear of old jeans and a floppy sweatshirt. She wasn't going to risk another charge from Grant of dressing provocatively.

Watching from her front window, Natalie saw his car turn into the courtyard on the dot of seven. All the same, when she opened the door to his knock, the sudden impact of his presence was so overwhelming that she could only stare up at him speechlessly. He was wearing a pale blue shirt, open at the neck, with the jacket of his light gray suit hitched on one finger at his shoulder. It struck her with a fresh shock that though Grant wasn't handsome in any conventional sense, he was the most devastatingly attractive man she had ever encountered.

"Aren't you going to invite me in, Natalie?" he inquired with a slow, lazy smile that seemed to stroke her skin.

"Er . . ." Ridiculously flustered, she stepped aside for him to pass. Strolling across the room with long, fluid strides, Grant stood for a moment at the rear window which looked out over her small paved patio, where she had a display of wallflowers and forget-me-nots in two rustic tubs. Beyond, on the canal, a pleasure launch was just coming into view.

"What a little oasis of peace and tranquillity this place is," he commented, turning back to face Natalie.

"Driving through that archway from the street, it's like entering another world. The whole pace of life here seems more easy and relaxed."

"We still have to battle for a living like everyone else," she pointed out testily. "Don't run away with the idea that we're a bunch of arty dilettantes."

"Did I suggest that? All the same . . ." Grant's dark eyes traveled slowly and savoringly over her slender figure in unhurried appraisal . . . long legs, slim hips encased in jeans; loose, shapeless sweatshirt which, even so, enticingly revealed the swell of her breasts. "All the same . . . I can't imagine that you need do much battling for a living."

Natalie bit back a sharp retort, deciding it would be wiser to let the innuendo pass. Pointing to the tube of plans, which now rested on her desk by the window, she said in a crisp voice, "That's what you came for."

Grant's gaze went to the two color-wash drawings also lying on the desktop, as she had known it must. He moved closer, studying them with interest. "The penthouse at Princess Dock?" he queried.

Natalie nodded, her heart thudding. "Just a couple of ideas I had for a treatment. I set them down on paper while they were fresh in my mind." She gave an elaborate shrug. "With amendments, they'll probably be usable somewhere else."

"They're first-rate," he commented. "You know that, don't you?"

"I'm quite pleased with them," she admitted.

He resumed his study of the drawings, then said, "Could you do more of this sort of thing, for some of the other apartments?"

"Why?" she asked cautiously.

"They might be useful to clinch a deal with a hesitant client . . . an example of how the apartments *could* look, given the right decorative treatment."

Natalie bristled furiously. "You've got some nerve!

You scorned my suggestion in your office, and now you're wheeling it out yourself as if it's your own brilliant idea. I told you, remember, that my work could help sell the apartments for you."

Grant held up a pacific hand. "Be fair, Natalie. I didn't know, then, what you were capable of. I figured you meant the sort of drawings that wouldn't convey much to a lay person. But these . . . they're superb."

"I guess I ought to be grateful for that," Natalie said wryly, careful to hide her excitement at this whiff of victory. "So, what exactly is your proposition?"

"How about if I commission you to do a series of sketches for . . . say, half a dozen apartments? My negotiators might find them useful, and if a client likes your ideas, you'll be put in touch to make a direct deal. Fair enough?"

Could she have hoped for more? But she still felt little claws of suspicion, and asked doubtfully, "No strings?"

He tilted his head. "Such as?"

"A *quid pro quo*, perhaps. A reward for your trouble . . . in kind."

Grant regarded her with an angry frown. "I don't need to hand out favors to get myself a love life."

"So all those women I've been hearing about just queue up for the privilege, do they?"

"Been hearing about from whom?" he inquired interestedly.

"Oh, people. . . ."

"You've discussed me?" He sounded smugly pleased.

Natalie bit her lip, vexed with herself for falling into such an easy trap. "Your name happened to crop up," she said offhandedly. "It was nothing important. Now, about this deal of ours . . ."

"You agree?"

"Why not?"

"You'll want to look over Princess Dock again," he stated. "When shall I take you?"

"There's no need for that," she protested. "I mean, one of your staff could—"

"I'll escort you myself," Grant cut across her decidedly. "We'll have lunch at the Hangman's Noose first, as we did before."

"Thanks, but I'd rather skip lunch, if you don't mind."

"I do mind." Why was it, she asked herself despairingly, that every glance from those dark eyes was like an erotic caress? "Give me one good reason, Natalie, why we shouldn't give such a pleasurable experience a rerun."

"Look where it led us," she returned bitterly. "I thought I'd spelled it out that I won't accept any conditions."

"Haven't I agreed? Ours will be a strictly no-strings relationship."

Natalie took a deep, shuddery breath, feeling her previous optimism drain away. "There isn't going to be any 'relationship' between us."

"Then how," he demanded with a twitch of his lips, "are we to do business together?"

"You know what I mean," she snapped.

Grant regarded her quizzically. "So, you're too prickly a feminist to let me buy you lunch again—right? Okay, there's a simple and acceptable way for you to square the account, Natalie. Since I'm here in your home and it's getting near time for dinner, you could offer to fix something for me with your own fair hands."

"No way," she responded fiercely.

"That's a most inhospitable attitude, Mrs. Kent."

A tempting picture formed in Natalie's mind, of herself and Grant seated at the small ceramic-topped table by the window, the room softly lamplit, the scent of wallflowers drifting in on the evening air. And outside, as the twilight deepened, reflections dancing on the dark water of the canal. She felt a sudden wave of longing, but it had to be resisted.

"Doesn't it occur to you," she said coldly, "that I might have other plans for dinner this evening?"

He looked penetratingly into her eyes. "Have you?"

"Well, not actually. But . . ." She hesitated, then unwisely tried another way out. "I've no food, anyway."

"Not even enough to throw into an omelet or whatever?"

Natalie gave him a reluctant nod. "I daresay I could scrape something up."

"That's great. Come on, then. I'll lend you a hand."

In the end she managed to pull together quite a decent meal. The refrigerator yielded a few mushrooms as a filling for omelets and a packet of frozen broccoli spears to garnish them. Luckily, there was even a can of beer she could offer him. She also produced crackers and a wedge of Brie cheese, plus a basket of fruit to set on the table.

"I've discovered yet another of your many talents," Grant said appreciatively when they were sitting down. "Not only have you an excellent brain—from eating so much fish, no doubt—plus fabulous looks and style, but you can whip up tempting food in no time flat. What more could a man ask for in a woman?"

"That's a sexist remark," Natalie rebuked him.

Grant quirked an eyebrow. "If by 'sexist' you mean acknowledging certain basic differences between male and female, then I plead guilty to being a sexist."

"I meant," she said explicitly, "that you were being condescending."

"On the contrary, I'm all admiration and respect for the role that women play in the modern world."

"So! It's admiration and respect you feel for all those beautiful blondes in your life, is it?"

"It's what I feel for you, Natalie," he replied suavely.

"Glad to hear it." She buttered a cracker. "It will help us confine our conversation to professional matters."

"Feeling admiration and respect," he pointed out dryly, "doesn't rule out other . . . more interesting emotions."

She threw him a defiant look across the small table. "Can we please get this straightened out once and for all? I'll be happy to work with you, but that's as far as it goes. Okay?"

"What a waste," he said with a rueful smile. "Some of the most successful working relationships are between people who're also good friends."

"Maybe. It's where being good friends can lead that I'm concerned about."

"Between consenting adults, who's to say where it should or shouldn't lead?"

"I, though, wouldn't be consenting," Natalie retorted.

"You were the other day, up on the rooftop at Princess Dock," he reminded her softly. "You insisted, in no uncertain terms, that your response had nothing whatever to do with luring me into engaging your services as an interior designer."

"That was the truth," Natalie flared indignantly.

"Which leaves us, doesn't it, with the alternative explanation. You let me kiss you simply and solely because you wanted me to kiss you."

"Pure garbage!" she protested. "If you recall, I objected most strongly."

"Eventually," he agreed with a mocking smile.

Flushing, she said feebly, "Well, anyway, the circumstances won't occur again."

"If you say so, Natalie."

"I do say so. No question."

"Then what are you worrying about? You'll be perfectly safe, won't you . . . letting me take you to lunch, being all alone with me at Princess Dock? Even being alone with me here in your home."

Natalie looked at him doubtfully. "I'm still not sure that I can trust you."

"Or is it," he inquired silkily, "that you can't trust yourself?"

"That's a stupid thing to say."

"Prove it," he challenged. "Have lunch with me tomorrow, and afterward we'll spend all the time you like looking around the warehouse. It will give you a chance to prove how totally immune you are to me."

She hesitated. "You said no strings, remember."

Grant frowned in sudden annoyance. "Listen, Natalie, I've made you a straight professional offer and you've accepted it. Okay? I'm not a man to go back on my word, and I don't slip in small-print clauses."

Natalie found her doubts ebbing away. She believed in Grant's sincerity, as far as work went. That didn't mean, of course, that he wouldn't try his luck with her again. But if he did—*when* he did—she could handle it as she'd handled similar situations in the past. It was crazy to be at loggerheads with the man who would henceforth be a close working associate. And she was honest enough to admit that she enjoyed Grant's company. Even the verbal sparring had been pleasurable, bringing with it a surge of adrenaline that seemed to set the blood dancing in her veins.

She crushed down the knowledge that she would be playing with fire. "Okay," she agreed, "I'll have lunch with you tomorrow."

Grant grinned cheerfully. "That's my girl!"

"I'm not your girl," she countered, "and I never shall be—as I thought I'd spelled out in words of one syllable."

Grant raised his glass to her in a mock salutation. "What a fighter you are. But you can't be right all the time, Natalie. Let's just wait and see how things work out, shall we?"

He helped her carry the dishes out to the kitchen and lingered there while she set about making coffee, standing so close that at times she couldn't avoid accidentally brushing against his arm. She was intensely aware of Grant, of the vibrant sensuality that emanated from his leanly muscular frame. When she reached in a high cupboard for a fresh packet of filter papers, she felt his warm breath stir the hair at her nape . . . just as on the warehouse roof in the moments before he'd kissed her. She froze into stillness, dreading his touch, yet aching for it with a kind of desperation.

It came slowly, at first just the gentle pressure of his warm, throbbing flesh against her slender length from shoulder to thigh. Shocked and dismayed at the rush of excitement that flooded through her, Natalie tried to make a sidestepping movement in the restricted space. But Grant's arms forestalled her, encircling her waist from behind. His hands moved up to cup the warm softness of her breasts, squeezing gently, his thumbs making lazy, teasing circles around each nipple, while his lips nuzzled into the fragrant silk cloud of her hair. Desperately she attempted to stay frozen, to be stiff and unyielding to this insidious assault, but her treacherous body refused to obey the dictates of her mind and she felt herself becoming soft and pliant, leaning back against his hard lean strength. A tremor ran through her and she had to stifle back a moan of pleasure. . . .

"The kettle's boiling," Grant pointed out in a low, throaty voice, and eased himself away from her.

Damn him . . . oh, damn him! Flushing with embarrassment, her movements made clumsy by her trembling response to him, Natalie resentfully set up the coffeepot and spooned ground coffee into the filter.

When the water from the kettle was trickling through, she forced herself to turn around and face him. By some miracle, she met his gaze unblinkingly, as if the last few moments hadn't happened.

"If you'll carry the tray through," she said in a brisk tone, "I'll bring the coffee when it's ready. Okay?"

"Right," he agreed affably. A couple of minutes later, he called from the living room, "Mind if I put on a record?" and before Natalie could answer, there came the soft throbbing beat of a film score, threaded through with an evocative theme on the clarinet. She regretted having left that particular disc on the turntable, but it was the sort of background music she liked to have on while at work. As she carried in the coffeepot, Grant was standing with his back to her, fingering a little terra-cotta plaque of a galloping horse. Unwillingly Natalie noted the way his broad shoulders narrowed to a trim waist, the slim cut of his trousers revealing a clear outline of his hips and thighs. With his head bent over the plaque, she could see the way his coppery dark hair grew to a point at the back of his neck. . . .

Grant swung around abruptly, and she knew from the little smile of satisfaction on his lips that he'd caught her staring. "This is good," he remarked, replacing the plaque on its stand. "It's skillfully modeled, expressing a sense of power."

"Riccardo did it," she told him, seizing her chance to get in a thrust.

Grant's eyes were suddenly hooded. "Ah, Riccardo! Do you see much of him?"

"A fairish bit," she answered, and added deliberately, "We're very good friends."

Grant made no comment, taking a spoonful of sugar and stirring his coffee thoughtfully. After a couple of sips, he sat down on the sofa and patted the place beside him encouragingly. Natalie pointedly chose an armchair instead. Nonetheless, across the several feet of space that separated them, she could feel his magnetism reaching out like a living force.

"Do you like this music?" she asked, dredging up something to say.

"Sure. It's marvelously atmospheric. Just the right sort of music for two people in our situation, don't you agree?"

"How do you make that out?" she asked warily.

He lifted one eyebrow. "Didn't you see the film?"

"I . . . I believe I did."

"Aren't you sure? I'd have said it's not the sort of film one easily forgets—a man and a woman caught up in a passionate involvement bigger than themselves."

Natalie shrugged, thinking it safer to make no comment. She felt almost too scared to open her mouth again, yet the stretching silence between them grew even more alarming.

When the record player finally clicked to a stop, Grant glanced at his wristwatch and said with a regretful smile, "That late! I really must be going. I have a planning meeting in the morning, and there's about five hours' preparatory work in my briefcase to be waded through first." He stood up, all six-foot-plus of him towering above her. "Thanks for the supper, Natalie, it was delicious."

She'd not wanted Grant to come in the first place, and all the time he was here she'd been willing him gone. Yet now the thought of him leaving was unbearably painful. As he stood looking down at her with a strange, questioning expression in his deep-set gray eyes, she was terrified by the strength of her longing to go to him and fold herself into his arms, to beg him to stay. She stood on legs that trembled, and forced herself to appear casually indifferent. "It sounds as if you've got a heavy schedule tomorrow."

"The morning I could do without, but from lunchtime on it will be pure, unadulterated pleasure." Grant retrieved his jacket from where he'd tossed it down on a chair. "I'll call for you at twelve-thirty, okay?"

"You don't need to fetch me," she began in quick protest, but Grant was adamant.

"Twelve-thirty," he stated. "I'll get my secretary to book our table at the Hangman's Noose for one o'clock."

Weakly nodding her agreement, she followed him across the room to see him out. At the door he halted and turned back to her, his dark eyes giving her a searching look that probed her innermost soul. Natalie halted too, standing stiff and tense, her emotions surging like a turbulent sea.

When Grant reached out for her, she jerked back with a clumsy, involuntary movement. But she didn't escape him, and she didn't really want to.

"I'm only going to kiss you good night," he murmured, his arms sliding around her waist. "You can't object to that."

"You said no strings," she protested. "You promised."

"Sure, no strings." He pulled her closer and smiled down into her eyes. "Listen, Natalie, we've got everything straightened out between us. We each know where we stand. Okay? You've provided me with a delicious dinner this evening, and now I'm saying thank you. No strings—not even the flimsiest strand of a spider's web."

"But—"

He silenced her objection by seizing her lips with his own in a warm, lingering kiss, while one finger traced a wildly erotic journey down the length of her spine. Natalie's body seemed to liquefy as she relaxed against him, and her own hands crept up to claw and tug at his muscled shoulders. The kiss deepened, drenching her senses, and she felt weak with longing. Grant's hands were now caressing the soft, yielding flesh of her buttocks, and a warm flood of yearning pulsed through her. When at last he let her go, a shivering sigh escaped her lips.

"Good night, sweet Natalie," he said in a low, husky voice, and lightly ran one fingertip down the petal-soft skin of her cheek. Then he was through the door, striding across the courtyard to his car.

Watching him, noting the easy grace of his stride and the confident way he held his tautly muscled body, Natalie felt a painful ache in her throat. Why did he have to be so devastatingly attractive? Why did it have to be this man, this self-confessed Casanova, who had the power to reach through to her deepest emotions in a way that no other man had ever done?

Chapter Three

*G*oing for the second time to the Hangman's Noose with Grant and sitting again at "their" corner table on the balcony had a sense of familiarity, a dangerous intimacy, that rang warning bells in Natalie's brain. She reminded herself firmly of her objective—a smooth, harmonious working relationship between them. She would ride along with Grant Kilmartin just so far as it suited her, and no farther. If he expected more than she was ready to give, he would find that he'd made a big error of calculation.

"What made you break away from your previous firm and set up the Kilmartin Development Corporation?" she asked him in a deliberately chatty way.

Grant's eyes met hers with disconcerting directness. "I could ask you much the same question, Natalie."

"I guess I needed to prove to myself that I was as competent as I thought I was."

"As competent as a man?"

"You're being sexist again," she pointed out crisply.

Ignoring that, he said, "Your reasons were similar to mine. But in my case there were certain . . . complications."

"Such as?"

He hesitated a moment, then said in a flat, neutral tone, "Such as the handicapping factor that I happened to be working for my father-in-law. That is to say, he was my father-in-law then."

It came as a relief that Grant was now being candid about his marriage, after his reticence the other day. Not willing to admit that she'd already garnered this piece of information about him, Natalie said with a questioning look, "You mean . . . ?"

"I mean that, like you, I'm divorced." He raised his wineglass to her, and she noticed how fragile it looked in his long, firm fingers. "Shall we drink to that, Natalie? Here's to us, two intelligent people who were clever enough to see marriage for the infernal trap it is, and get out from under before we were totally destroyed."

She pointedly left her glass where it was on the table. "You sound bitter, Grant."

He gave her a small twisted smile that made her heart lurch. "Are you going to tell me that you came through the marriage experience quite unscathed? No shattered illusions?"

"I try not to think about my marriage," Natalie replied with a shrug. "It's past history. Besides, I have more important things to focus on these days, building my career."

"But you can't be so one-track-minded that you manage without . . . diversions?" His dark eyes were probing. "It didn't look that way, from what I saw at your studio the other day."

She regarded him freezingly. "Is this any concern of yours?"

"Apologies! But I'll remind you, Natalie, that it was you who started out along this line of conversation, not me. Still, if you prefer to regard your love life as too personal to be discussed . . . fair enough. We'll leave it until we get better acquainted."

"Which isn't going to happen," she stated firmly. "Not in the way you mean."

"I shan't abandon hope yet, Natalie. That's for sure. To date I've established that you're not the cold, frigid type. In fact, you responded to me in a way that makes me feel very optimistic."

"Just because I was stupid enough to let you kiss me on a couple of occasions?" she said scornfully. "I hope your construction projects aren't built on such flimsy foundations."

"My construction projects," he said evenly, "are required to be rather more enduring than a love affair. All the same, I think I have reasonable grounds for confidence with you, and I view the time ahead with enormous pleasure." His dark eyes took on a look of melting tenderness. "You are very beautiful, Natalie."

"I wish you wouldn't say things like that," she muttered uneasily.

"Why shouldn't I pay you compliments?"

"Because . . ." She paused, and swallowed hard. "You seem to be under the mistaken impression that you can coax me into having an affair with you."

He quirked an inquiring eyebrow. "Aren't you just a little bit tempted?"

If only he knew how desperately she was tempted. "Even if I were," she said in a resolute voice, adding hastily, "which I'm not, I wouldn't allow myself to give way to anything so . . . so ill-judged."

Grant smiled at her blithely. "According to Oscar Wilde, the only way to rid yourself of temptation is to yield to it."

"Oscar Wilde was a cynic."

"Which is just another way of saying that he was a realist."

"If you really believe that," Natalie returned acidly, "you must have a very distorted view of the world."

"I have a pretty fair grasp of what makes the world tick," he countered. "Most people deceive themselves all along the line—like you're doing right now. It would be far better to look the facts plainly in the face, Natalie."

"What facts?" she demanded.

Grant gave her a long, considering look. "Fact one, you and I are very attracted to each other. Fact two, we've both had romantic illusions knocked out of us by a failed marriage, which gives us a common starting point. Fact three, no career can succeed on the basis of all work and no play."

"Play!" she echoed in a scathing voice. "Is that how you regard your relationships with women?"

"Why not?" he inquired blandly.

"It seems so horribly . . . uncommitted."

"Oh, commitment!" He hefted his shoulders in a shrug. "That's what marriage is supposed to be all about, isn't it? And look where it's landed us both. I prefer to take my pleasures lightly, Natalie. And before you chew me out, I don't mean selfishly or uncaringly— merely without being anchored down."

"It amazes me," she said, putting bite into her tone, "that you can find enough women prepared to accept your unpalatable terms."

"I seem to have no problem," he drawled.

"Never a failure?"

His smile was maddeningly complacent. "Let's say that I enjoy a good success rate."

"This is where the graph takes a dive, then. You have a total failure to record."

"That," he said smoothly, "remains to be seen, Natalie."

"It's a foregone conclusion."

"You think? I'll remind you that you're having lunch with me for the second time this week. I'd say that was making good progress, wouldn't you?"

Natalie threw him a furious look across the table. "You can't honestly imagine that the price of a couple of lunches will buy you . . ."

"Will buy me what?" he prompted, when she didn't finish.

"You know very well what I mean."

Grant calmly broke off a piece of French bread and dabbed on butter. When he spoke, his voice was low-pitched and caressing. "If I thought that you carried a price tag, Natalie, I wouldn't be interested."

"The tag I carry," she told him forcefully, "reads *Hands Off, Don't Touch.*"

He laughed. "That makes you sound like a dusty museum exhibit, which is something you most definitely aren't. You're a warm-blooded, vibrant woman, Natalie." As he met her eyes, all trace of jokiness was gone, and the intent look he gave her set her pulses leaping. Luckily she had sufficient command of her wits to recognize it as a hazardous moment.

"I'm really looking forward to planning decorative treatments for Princess Dock," she said with forced brightness. "When would you want the preliminary sketches?"

Grant made a face at her. "What a workaholic you are! But you can go easy on this job, Natalie. It'll be months before I'm ready to offer any of the apartments for sale."

White puffs of cloud chased across an azure sky as they fetched the keys from the watchman's cottage and strolled the short distance to Princess Dock. It was pleasantly warm, a good day to be viewing such a bleak site. Grant had once again brought along the architectural plans, and Natalie decided that she would make a detailed study of the two corner apartments on each floor that would be nearest the river, those with the best views. Trying to ignore the blood-stirring magnetism of Grant's presence, she became briskly professional as she moved around, peering through gaps in the boarded-up windows to judge what the outlook there would be. Ideas seethed in her brain, and she jotted down a series of cryptic notes and thumbnail sketches on the pad she'd brought in her shoulder bag.

Presently Grant left her to get on, saying that he wanted to go to the dockside and check out the structural condition of the lock gates.

Time went by and Natalie became so engrossed in what she was doing that she didn't hear his footsteps remounting the stairs. Suddenly she turned around and saw him standing at the top of the stairs, watching her with his dark, penetrating gaze. How long he'd been quietly observing her, she didn't know, but there was a deeply thoughtful expression on his face. Their glances met, and she felt a powerless captive in the grasp of his eyes.

As if mesmerized, she watched him coming slowly toward her till he was very close. He reached out one hand and ran his fingertips down the curve of her cheek in a delicate caress, just as he'd done the previous night; then he leaned forward and put his mouth to hers in a long, drowning kiss. Without taking his lips away, he slid his arms around her and pulled her against him, molding her soft body to his lean length. Natalie wanted to struggle free, but with a sense of dizzy helplessness she felt her resistance ebbing away as the kiss deepened. With a thirsty passion he coaxed her lips apart to permit the entry of his probing tongue, which darted teasingly around her mouth in a way that she found unbelievably exciting. It awoke needs and longings that had lain dormant for years, and she was shocked at the sudden surge of desire that filled her whole being. Tears pressed out from beneath her closed lids—tears of frustration at her own weakness.

Grant became aware of the tears and immediately released his tight hold. He held her a little from him, his eyes searching her face.

"You're crying!" There was deep puzzlement in his voice. "Surely being kissed isn't such a disaster?"

"You don't understand," she choked.

"Right, I don't!" Turning away, he asked in a cold, abrupt voice, "How soon will you be through here?"

Natalie said unhappily, "There's no point in my taking any more notes."

"You have all the data you need?"

"No, but . . . well, you . . . you can't still want me to do this job."

She heard his angry rasp of breath. "Why in the hell not?"

"I wouldn't want to hold you to our deal, in the circumstances," she faltered. "If you prefer to jettison the whole idea . . ."

"I'm not in the habit of going back on my word, Natalie. When I say something, it's for real. Anyway, I like what I've seen of your work, and I'm confident that you'll do a great job for me."

"And . . . and you accept now that there can't be anything else between us?"

He was silent for what seemed like an unendurably long time. Then, instead of answering her question, he said, "I'll leave you to finish off. I'll be downstairs when you're ready to go. Just give me a shout."

Natalie heard his footsteps clattering down the stairs . . . one flight, two, three, growing fainter. All of a sudden she felt terribly isolated and alone. It was an effort to concentrate. Her thoughts kept drifting back to those tension-charged moments when Grant had kissed her. Undeniably, her body ached with a longing to feel again the warm intimacy of his embrace, the exciting, erotic sensation his lips and tongue had aroused. But in her mind she was furious about what had happened. She reproached herself bitterly for mishandling the situation. A woman her age should find it possible to deal with a sexual prowler like Grant Kilmartin. No matter how clever his tactics, she should be able to maneuver out of dangerous corners with a flip remark.

When at last she went downstairs, she found Grant in the big cobbled courtyard, sitting on a bollard and moodily staring out across the dock basin. He heard her footsteps, and turned.

"All set?" he asked unsmilingly.

She nodded. "I can't usefully do any more at this stage."

Grant locked the warehouse and the outer gates, and returned the keys. In his car, he queried tersely, "Straight home now?"

"Yes . . . but you needn't take me all the way. Drop me off at the nearest Underground."

"We've been through this scene before," he snapped, a flare of impatience in his eyes. "I'll drive you home, Natalie. But I won't come in today. I have to get back to the office."

"As you wish." She sat quietly as he nosed the car through the narrow dockland streets. After a few minutes she asked, "About these architectural drawings . . . may I hang on to them for a little while? I could have them photocopied and send you the originals back, if that's okay?"

"You keep them," Grant said crisply. "That's a spare set." Silence. Then, "I'll leave it to you to get in touch when you have something to show me."

"Very well." The thought that he wouldn't be contacting her in the meantime filled Natalie with a strange despondency. Everything seemed suddenly pointless. Till now her career had been the driving force in her life, each new job, each new achievement bringing her satisfying challenges and rewards. It was all very well to keep forging ahead, she thought gloomily, but there had to be an end in view. Was success for its own sake a worthwhile goal in life?

Grant swung the car through the brick archway at Chandler's Wharf and drew to a halt in the courtyard. He didn't switch the motor off. "Right, then," he said in a brittle voice, "I'll expect to hear from you when your drawings are ready."

"It shouldn't be very long," she said as she opened the car door.

"There's no rush. Take your time." His tone was distant, uninterested.

"Well . . . thanks again for the ride."

"A pleasure." He made it sound the very reverse. "By the way, we haven't yet agreed on your fee."

"Let's leave it for the moment," she said hastily. "I'm sure we needn't get into a fight about that."

"Not a very professional attitude to take," he commented dryly. "Still, if that's what you want . . ."

"Yes, it is."

Grant shifted the car into gear and released the hand brake. "Be seeing you sometime." It sounded, Natalie thought unhappily, as if he didn't care how long it was before he saw her again.

"Natalie, it's so good of you to come at such short notice," Lady Aston greeted her. "I need to have a chat with you before you proceed any further with the Barbican apartment."

Natalie sighed inwardly, guessing what was coming, and followed her client through to the drawing room. This block of mansion flats in Maida Vale dated from the last century, reflecting the more gracious Victorian era in its large rooms, high corniced ceilings, and ornately carved marble fireplaces. Celia Aston, she mused, would have felt very much at home in the building's heyday—a dedicated wife and mother who saw her role as meekly submissive to her husband's dictates. Accordingly, she spent a great deal of money on clothes, but each expensive garment lost a vital something on her plump, shapeless figure, and Natalie guessed that Celia would have been far more comfortable in a well-worn blouse and skirt. There was a warmhearted simplicity about her that Natalie found appealing, and fortunately, Lady Aston seemed to like her in return. "I feel at ease with you, Natalie, dear," she had once confided. "We talk the same sort of language. Some of your professional colleagues can be so forceful and hectoring. Like the man who designed the interiors of our house in Hampshire. He made it clear to me that he knew best what ought to be done, and that my suggestions were unwelcome."

Now, seated on the huge tapestry-covered sofa, Natalie tried to help Celia over her present embarrassment. "I take it, Lady Aston, you're going to tell me that the Barbican apartment is off?"

"I'm afraid so, my dear." She sighed unhappily. "I really was beginning to think that this time we could go ahead, but then yesterday my husband discovered that one of his executive directors, someone quite newly appointed to the board of Aston Financial Holdings, lives in the adjoining flat. Matthew felt it wouldn't do at all for the chairman and a fairly junior director to be next-door neighbors."

"I suppose Sir Matthew has a point there," Natalie conceded with a rueful little smile. "It's lucky he found out in time."

Celia smiled back in relief and gratitude. "You're always so understanding, Natalie. It seems such a dreadful shame that the lovely ideas you'll have planned for me will not be put into effect. I still want to see them, of course, and maybe you can adapt them to fit in with whatever place we finally settle on for our new London home."

They spent several minutes looking through the presentation portfolio Natalie had brought with her, and at each sketch, together with its accompanying snippets of wallpaper and fabric, Lady Aston was warm in her praise.

"Oh, they're all so beautiful," she said with a regretful sigh when she'd seen everything. "I can't tell you how sorry I am that once again it has all been a waste of time for you."

"I can't grumble, Lady Aston. You pay me very well."

"Ah, but the money side doesn't mean that much to you, does it, dear? You're like me, and you understand that the really important thing is to have a sense of satisfaction in whatever you do. But, alas, that isn't always possible in life." With a disconcerting switch, she went on, "When are you going to set about finding yourself another husband?"

After a stunned moment, Natalie said carefully, "I'm not at all sure that I want to get married again. Certainly not for the time being, anyway."

"Oh, but these are the best years of your life, Natalie, dear. Don't let them slip away."

"I'm fully occupied with building my career, Lady Aston."

The gentle blue eyes became wistful. "I envy you that. It must be a source of great satisfaction to you to make a success of something entirely by your own efforts."

"Indeed it is!" Natalie concurred. "I have a marvelous feeling of independence."

"All the same," Lady Aston put in sagely, "for a woman, true love is better than all the independence in the world."

"And a lot more difficult to come by," Natalie pointed out. "I've discovered that the hard way."

The older woman looked at her sorrowfully. "I know I have no right to be talking to you like this, but I do feel we're friends. So please, my dear, don't allow the fact that you made one mistake make you bitter about marriage itself." Rising to her feet, she added hurriedly, "End of lecture! Now I'll go and make a pot of tea. I shall only be a moment."

"Can I do anything to help?"

"No, thank you, dear, I have everything ready. I only need to make the tea and wheel the trolley in."

Left alone, Natalie rose and wandered around the room, admiring a set of Japanese flower paintings on the wall. From things Lady Aston had told her, and what she had further surmised, she knew that this apartment had marked a triumphant upgrading of Matthew Aston's status at the time he and his wife had taken a lease here a few years back. Since then, they had acquired a thirty-room mansion in Hampshire, plus a villa in the south of France. And now it had become a problem to find a new London home that was a sufficiently accurate mirror of his lofty position in the world of high finance. Sir Matthew had sprung from humble origins, Lady Aston had confided; one of a large family living in the East End of London, his father being a street trader with a fruit barrow. He had started his working life in a very junior capacity with a firm of insurance brokers. He and Celia had first met when he was promoted to section supervisor in the department where she was a typist. And now he was boss man of his very own business empire. Presumably success had brought him enormous satisfaction, if not happiness; but what about his wife? Natalie knew that Celia Aston was devoted to her husband, and very proud of him for having achieved so much. But somehow happiness had eluded her. She was like a fish out of water in the glittering world in which they now moved.

Natalie's wandering had brought her to one of the tall windows, draped with green brocade curtains. Across the street, hoardings had been erected around some buildings which were being renovated. A large signboard in blue and white proclaimed that this was a project of the Kilmartin Development Corporation. The sight of Grant's name spelled out in large letters brought a sudden speeding of Natalie's pulse rate. She recalled him saying that he had a scheme near completion in the Maida Vale area . . . a shopping arcade, she seemed to remember.

"It will be really lovely when it's all finished," came Celia Aston's voice from behind her.

Natalie spun around, jolted out of her musings. "It . . . it must make a lot of noise and dust for you while the work is under way."

"Well, yes, but it's in a good cause. Before anything was started, the developer invited all the local residents to a get-together in order to explain his plans, and he asked for our suggestions. He's bringing all our nice little neighborhood shops together in a single covered arcade. I think it's going to look most attractive, and it will make shopping so convenient, especially when it's wet." She sighed, and a sorrowful expression came into her round face. "Of course, we shan't be here much longer. I'm going to miss all these little shops when we leave. Particularly my butcher . . . such a nice helpful man. Oh, and the baker, too. He sells really good home-baked bread. You can't get that in many places these days, can you?"

"You certainly can't!" Natalie paused, then said offhandedly, "So you met Grant Kilmartin?"

Lady Aston nodded. "A very pleasant, good-looking man. I thought how competent he was, so patient and ready to explain every detail. Do you know him, Natalie?"

"Er . . . slightly."

The door banged open to admit a girl of about seventeen. She wore grimy, tattered blue jeans with a top of some curious furry material; her hair, a warm honey color, could have looked nice if she'd taken the trouble to use a brush and comb, but it was in a tangled mess that looked none too clean. The hostile expression on her face was habitual, Natalie guessed, and not directed at anyone in particular.

"Oh, hello, Jodi," said Celia Aston, glancing up from pouring tea with an uncertain smile. "This is Mrs. Kent. Natalie, my daughter, Jodi. If you want some tea, dear, perhaps you'll fetch another cup."

"Tea!" The girl's tone was thick with scorn. But that didn't prevent her, Natalie noted amusedly, from gathering up a handful of chocolate cookies from the delicate china platter. "I want to borrow your car," she announced belligerently, her mouth full.

"Don't be silly, darling, how can you? Until you've passed your driving test, you need to have someone experienced with you, and I can't possibly come at the moment."

"Steve will be with me."

"Steve?" her mother queried anxiously.

Jodi gave an impatient shrug, as if she'd given all the explanations any reasonable person could expect. "Well, are you going to let me have the car or not?"

A visible shudder passed through Celia Aston's plump body. It looked as if she were fighting for courage to stand up to her daughter. "No, darling," she said quietly, "I'm afraid you can't have it, not to go off with some young man I've never even met. Whatever would your father say?"

"Oh, dear, we mustn't upset Daddy, must we?" The girl sneered. "Why do you always shelter behind him, Mother? Don't you have a mind of your own?" With that Jodi was gone, barely having acknowledged Natalie's presence.

"Girls can be so difficult at that age," Celia muttered apologetically. "So headstrong and rebellious." She sighed deeply as she handed Natalie a cup of tea. "If only her brother were still alive, things might have been so different."

"Her brother?"

Celia rose to cross to an escritoire on which stood several silver-framed photographs, and passed one of them to Natalie. It showed a fresh-faced young man with fair hair and blue eyes, together with a younger, schoolgirl version of Jodi. He had an arm thrown around her shoulders and she was gazing up at him adoringly.

"Keith was such a lovely boy." Celia's voice shook with emotion. "He was never any problem to his father and me, nothing but a joy to us. And Jodi thought the world of him. Everybody did."

"Yes, I'm sure they did," Natalie murmured, then asked tentatively, "When did he . . . ?"

"Two years ago . . . a mountaineering accident in Austria. Keith had such a love of adventure, yet he never acted in a foolhardy way. He died rescuing another climber who was in difficulties."

"You must be very proud of him, Lady Aston."

"Extremely proud. He was a highly intelligent boy, too. Matthew says he would have made an ideal successor to take over from him when the time eventually comes. But when Keith was killed . . . well, we did hope that Jodi might like the idea of joining the firm, but she's made it very clear that she's not interested. I don't believe that she'll care two straws what happens to Aston Financial Holdings after her father gives up. She seems to have a contempt for everything he's worked so hard all his life to achieve."

Was that the root of the trouble, Natalie found herself wondering, that Jodi felt pressured? Did she resent her parents expecting her to act the filial role that had been mapped out for her brother? A brother, moreover, who had acquired saintly qualities since his death. No flesh-and-blood young man could have been such a paragon.

"Your daughter is just going through an awkward stage," Natalie ventured by way of comfort. "I'm sure she'll change as she gets older."

"I do hope so." Celia shook her head despairingly.

"If only Jodi could find a really nice, *wholesome* young man, instead of the dreadful types she seems to be attracted to at the moment."

Meeting the right man, Natalie thought ruefully, seemed to be Lady Aston's universal panacea for women. Celia seized on the faintest whiff of romance like a dog seizes a bone. She began to talk now about a niece of her husband's who had just become engaged to a clever young surgeon at Barts Hospital.

"I'll have to start thinking about a wedding present for them," she said, puckering her forehead. "It's always so difficult to know what to give, isn't it? Do you have any bright ideas, Natalie?"

This was a chance, Natalie thought, to put in a good word for Diane. "I have a neighbor at Chandler's Wharf who does very beautiful glass engraving, Lady Aston. You might like to consider something of hers."

Celia clapped her hands delightedly. "Now, that's a really splendid idea. If you recommend her, then she must be good." She made a note of Diane's name and phone number before Natalie took her leave.

After several days of concentrated work on the commission from Grant—because she seemed unable to focus her attention on any other job—her sketches for the various apartments, together with paste-ups of fabric and wallpaper samples, were complete. And very effective they looked, too, Natalie complimented herself as she assembled these into her usual presentation portfolio. Yet now that the time had come to show Grant what she'd done, she felt ridiculously nervous. She had to force herself to pick up the phone and punch out the number of his office. When connected with his secretary, she faltered, "This is Natalie Kent. I was wondering if it might be possible for me to see Mr. Kilmartin this afternoon."

"I'd better check with him first, Mrs. Kent. He has a rather tight schedule today."

Having screwed up her courage, Natalie felt a stupid panic at the thought that their meeting might be delayed until tomorrow or later. "Will you tell him," she said, "that I have the sketches for the Princess Dock development ready to show him."

The few seconds she was kept waiting seemed like an hour. By the time the secretary was back on the phone, Natalie's throat felt tight with strain.

"Mrs. Kent?"

"What does he say?" she demanded.

"Could you make it five o'clock? Mr. Kilmartin will be clear of his other appointments by then, so he'll be able to give you more time."

"Right, I'll be there."

Putting down the phone, she found that her heart was thudding in nervous anticipation. She pondered long and hard about what to wear. It mustn't be an outfit that Grant could possibly construe as provocative. Finally she decided on a cream skirt and bronze silk blouse worn with her velvet blazer that matched the rich chestnut of her hair. Anxious not to be late, she emerged from the Underground station at Trafalgar Square fifteen minutes early and had to wander around killing time. Fat pigeons strutted importantly across her path, street photographers snapped the sightseers, and children pranced gleefully in the drifts of spray from the fountains. Lord Nelson atop his tall column watched over the scene benignly, guarded by Landseer's four huge stone lions.

It was time to get moving. The short walk across the street to Grant's office left Natalie strangely breathless. The friendly receptionist she'd met before passed her on to Grant's secretary, who asked her to sit down for a moment, as he was on the phone.

Three minutes ticked by, then the inner door opened and Grant emerged. As on that very first occasion, the sight of him caused her heart to miss a beat. Even though his image had scarcely been absent from her mind for a single instant, his incredible attractiveness came as a fresh assault to her senses.

"Hi, Natalie," he said, giving her a brief, abstracted nod. He walked over to the secretary's desk and tossed down a sheaf of letters. "All signed, Tessa. But I have a feeling that you miscalculated the conversion figure on the Allbright contract. Just check it again before you mail it. Then you can get away."

"Thanks, GK."

He turned to Natalie and smiled; but it was a polite, impersonal smile. "Come through, will you? You're a fast worker, that's for sure. I hadn't expected to see you this soon."

Too soon, was he implying? Did she appear overly keen to see him again? She followed Grant through to his office, fumbling awkwardly with the black tapes that fastened her portfolio. "These are only rough, of course," she said defensively. "That's what we agreed, wasn't it?"

"Sure." When she laid open the portfolio to expose the first sketch, he didn't even glance at it, but continued to study her face intently as if trying to see through her skull. Natalie found it unnerving and felt her cheeks flood with warm color. At length Grant lowered his gaze, saying, "Right, then, let's see what you've come up with."

He leafed through the pages, pausing a few moments at each sketch. Watching him, Natalie noticed the frown that dented his forehead, while his lips were pressed together in a hard, straight line. Her heart plunged. He was disappointed, that was evident. But what more had he anticipated? she thought with a spurt of anger. Without being able to tailor her designs to the tastes and idiosyncrasies of specific individuals, there was inevitably a certain impersonal quality about them, and she couldn't be expected to do more than indicate the sort of treatments that might be used. Yet, humiliatingly, she knew that Grant's approval of her work was far more important to her than whatever money and professional prestige she would gain from the Princess Dock project. Please, please, she prayed, let him not be too disappointed.

At long last Grant closed the portfolio and held it edge-up on the desk, his fingers gripping the covers together. He looked away from her as he spoke, avoiding her eyes. "You don't need me to tell you that these are good, Natalie. I'm impressed."

"Oh, I'm so glad you like them." Relief flooded through her and her spirits were suddenly zinging. Playing it cool, she said with a laugh, "I thought for a nasty moment, from the expression on your face, that you hated them."

"How could I?" He was still frowning. "It's just such a damn pity that . . ."

Again she was pricked by needles of alarm. "What's a pity?"

"Oh . . . nothing." Grant looked at her, then gave a quick smile. "Honestly, Natalie, they're great. If you handle every assignment you're given so competently, and so quickly, I don't see how you can fail to succeed in a big way."

"I'm going to try, anyway. This Princess Dock job will mean a great deal to my professional rating, I don't mind admitting."

"But, Natalie . . ." He broke off, and the expression in his dark eyes was unreadable. Then quickly he added, "I'd like you to have dinner with me tonight."

"No!" she said sharply. "I don't want anything of that sort. You know I don't."

"It would give me a lot of pleasure."

"That's not the point. We just have a business deal, Grant, and that's how I prefer to keep it."

With an impatient snatch of breath, he put out his hands to grip her by the shoulders, and looked deep into her eyes. "Listen, Natalie. Our business deal is something quite apart. I commissioned you to do some sketches for me, and you've done them—superbly, as I guessed you would. They're delivered now, and they'll be paid for. Inviting you to have dinner with me is totally unrelated."

"But I can't separate my life into different compartments," she objected, dizzily conscious of the warm pressure of his fingers.

"You don't make any distinction between work and leisure?" he asked incredulously.

Natalie looked away from him, confused. "Not . . . not when the same person is involved."

"You're denying me your company this evening for no other reason than we've had a business deal. Is that logical?"

"It's just the way I feel," she persisted.

Grant put his lean fingers beneath her chin, tilting her face so that she had to look at him. "I can't accept that. Suppose, instead of us meeting when you called at this office the other day, we'd met at a party or through a mutual friend. You'd accept a dinner date with me then, wouldn't you?"

"Perhaps," she hedged.

"Only perhaps?" His eyes held her gaze entrapped.

"Well, yes, I suppose. I'd have no particular reason to refuse, would I?"

"And you haven't now. Forget about our business deal, Natalie. Let's start over and pretend that we met in some totally different way. So . . . will you have dinner with me this evening, Natalie Kent?"

She felt torn in two. An inner voice warned her that another step forward in their relationship would carry

her beyond the point of no return. There was still time
to be firm and say no, to back away from danger. But
the prospect of spending the evening with Grant was
breathlessly tempting. How could it really matter, she
argued with herself, if she just went out this once with
him? How could it matter if she indulged in a light
flirtation with him, as she'd done with several men
these past few years? She was a mature woman, for
heaven's sake, not an inexperienced teenager. She
surely ought to know how far she could safely allow a
situation to develop, and stop it there. Grant couldn't
blame her for drawing a line, because she'd made her
viewpoint plain to him from the start.

Her hesitant wavering was answer enough to his
question. "There's a riverboat restaurant on the
Thames at Henley," he said briskly. "It's the perfect
setting for a balmy spring evening."

"Oh, but . . ."

He waited a moment, then inquired sardonically,
"What's your objection this time?"

"Isn't Henley rather a long way to go just for
dinner?"

"We have the whole evening before us. It won't take
long to get there on the motorway."

"But I'm not dressed for anywhere fancy."

He gave her a leisured scrutiny that sent little shivers
skittering across her skin. "You look fine to me,
Natalie. More than fine . . . very beautiful and very
desirable. But then, you never look anything else."

"Please . . ." she protested.

"Beg pardon," he said with mock humility. "I forgot
that paying you compliments has been declared ille-
gal." His grin was irresistible, and Natalie couldn't help
being won over. It was as if he were treating her as a
fellow conspirator against her other, primmer self.
"Come on, let's be off."

From the instant he took hold of her arm to escort

her out, Natalie felt as though she were living in a
dream. A dream, she tried to remind herself sternly,
that couldn't possibly have a happy ending. As they
sped along the motorway, she sat back savoring the rich
timbre of Grant's voice, and covertly from behind her
lashes she watched his profile, noting the firm molding
of his cheekbone and the taut line of his jaw.

In no time, it seemed, they had reached the quayside
where the riverboat was tied up. They parked the car
and went aboard. While they were served cocktails at a
small table under a striped deck awning, the sleek,
gleaming white vessel slipped from its moorings and
began the evening cruise, moving between the summer-
lush riverbanks with only the faintest throb of its
engines. Ahead, the water was like a sheet of ham-
mered bronze in the rays of the westering sun.

"How beautiful it is," Natalie said with a sigh of
contentment. "I've just realized . . . this is the first
time I've ever sailed on the River Thames."

Grant turned to look at her, and tutted. "For shame!
How long have you lived in London?"

"All my life," she confessed. "My parents' house was
near Hampstead Heath. Several times, I remember, my
mother and I talked about doing a river trip during the
school holidays, but somehow we never did."

"That's typical," Grant scoffed. "Born-and-bred
Londoners don't trouble to get to know their own city.
Whereas me . . . living abroad as I did with my folks,
when we happened to come to London, we acted like
regular tourists and did the sights."

"So you reckon you know London better than I
do—huh?"

"Try me. What about Westminster Abbey and St.
Paul's Cathedral . . . been inside them?"

"Oh, yes. We did both those places very thoroughly
on school outings."

"St. Bartholomew-the-Great, the oldest church in London?"

"Got me there."

"Petticoat Lane market on a Sunday morning?"

"Negative again. But we went to the Zoo, and the Tower of London, and the Science Museum," she reeled off. "How about you?"

"I remember them all well." He grinned. "Now let's get trickier. The Soane Museum at Lincoln's Inn Fields?"

"Do you mind, I'm a designer," she reminded him. "Naturally I've been *there,* several times. It's a gorgeous source of inspiration."

"The Wallace Collection?"

"Check," she said triumphantly. "How about the Victoria and Albert Museum? You could spend weeks in that vast place."

"I have done . . . hours anyway. Now, then, cricket at the Oval? Bet I've beaten you there."

Natalie granted another point to him, but countered hopefully, "Tennis at Wimbledon?"

"I never quite got around to Wimbledon," he finally conceded. "So that's a treat in store. How about me getting tickets for this year's tournament, and we'll go together?"

"We'll have to see." Natalie smiled evasively, but she found the thought of a day at Wimbledon with Grant was very appealing.

"Which means yes," he claimed. "I'm going to hold you to that. Now, shall we go and eat?"

They made their way down the carpeted companionway to the restaurant on the lower deck. They were shown to a window table, from where Natalie could see a red-roofed village set among trees, dominated by the squat tower of a Norman church.

"No doubt you'll be wanting fish," Grant teased as

they studied the elaborate menu. "Perhaps they could cast a line over the side and haul in something fresh for you."

Natalie settled for a *salade niçoise,* followed by duckling cooked with oranges and ginger, and Grant chose iced melon and a rump steak. Then he called for the wine list, saying, "It's got to be champagne this evening."

"Why?" she queried, liking the idea.

"Because," he said, meeting her eyes across the table, "nothing less would do for such a special occasion."

It *was* a special occasion, Natalie had to agree, a very special occasion. There was a strange, uncanny quality about what was happening to her. Never before had she felt so totally in tune with anyone. It was as if she and Grant were the only two real people in the whole world, and the other diners at tables all around them were no more than cardboard cut-out figures.

The champagne arrived. The waiter popped the cork with a flourish and poured the foaming wine into tall tulip glasses.

"Let's drink to us, Natalie, to you and me," Grant said in a low, throbbing voice. "To what the future holds for us."

A tremor shivered through her. "But I don't . . ."

"There you go again," he said with a weary sigh. "Get this into your head, my dear sweet girl. I'm not trying to hustle you into anything you don't want. Right?"

But that, she thought forlornly, was the whole point at issue. What *did* she want from Grant? Her emotions were in a state of crazy confusion, her physical responses to him pulling one way and her mental reservations in the opposite direction. It seemed so feeble after all these years of avoiding any emotional entanglement to weakly give way to the sensual longings that

Grant had aroused in her, yet reason and logic could come up with no convincing argument why she should go on denying herself the joy of sexual fulfillment.

Smiling tremulously, she reached out hesitant fingers and gripped the slender wineglass, raising it to her lips. "Here's to *you*, Grant!"

"To *us!*" he insisted, and smiled deep into her eyes.

Chapter Four

*L*ater, they danced on deck under the striped canvas awning. The music, from a combo of keyboard, double bass and drums, throbbed a slow, sensual beat, and the balmy night air seemed filled with perfumed magic.

"You're so lovely, Natalie," Grant murmured, and touched his lips to the petal-soft lobe of her ear. "So very desirable."

A tremor ran down her spine. She tried to keep the shakiness from her voice with a flip retort. "Don't push your luck, chum."

She knew without looking that a smile lit Grant's lean, angled features. He was growing too confident, she thought despairingly, altogether too sure of her. But here on the boat she felt helplessly trapped, forced to wait until the river cruise ended, unable to break things up by pleading tiredness and the need to get home. Was that why he'd chosen to bring her here tonight?

When at last they were ashore again, they walked the short distance to where his car was parked. But when they were seated, Grant didn't start the engine. Instead, he leaned across and pulled her into his arms. With a little half-articulate whimper, Natalie found herself melting against him, eager to meet the demanding claims of his mouth as he lowered his lips to hers.

His kiss was intoxicating, sending darts of excitement zinging through her and making the blood surge dizzily to her head. Softly, insidiously, his lips forced hers apart and his tongue speared in to dart under and over her own tongue and sip the nectar of her mouth.

"Oh, Natalie, you're so sweet . . . you taste so good."

Now his questing lips began to roam her face . . . dropping butterfly kisses on her closed eyelids, outlining the shape of her brow and trailing down the curve of her cheek to the smooth tender skin of her throat, while his fingers caressed the nape of her neck beneath the silken curtain of her hair. Slipping his hand in under the lapel of her velvet blazer, he let it move down in sweet exploration until it came to rest enclosing her quivering soft flesh in a firm, warm cradle. Through the silk fabric of her blouse he sensuously stroked the nipple with tiny feathery flicks of his thumb to a peak of tingling hardness. Natalie didn't even try to stop him, knowing it was useless. Instead, she responded joyfully, arching against him and delighting in the blissful sensations that were filling her whole body.

At long last Grant released her enough to say breathlessly, "Sweet darling Natalie. When we get back to Chandler's Wharf you aren't going to make me say good night, are you?"

"Of course I am." Her voice came out with shrill intensity.

He gave a deep, shuddering sigh of resignation. "Okay. You told me not to push my luck, and I won't." Then, "What shall we do tomorrow evening?"

"I . . . I can't see you tomorrow, Grant."

"Can't?" he questioned.

"Won't, then."

In the darkness she saw the glitter of his eyes. "If I were to ask you for, say, one evening next week . . . would you accept?"

"Perhaps."

"So what's the difference?" he demanded. "Why

waste all the days in between when we could be together?"

Natalie shifted on the leather seat, moving away from him. Staring down at her lap, nervously smoothing her skirt, she said, "You've got to understand, Grant, that you and I . . . well, we're not going anyplace. It's been a lovely evening, I've really enjoyed it, but this is where we ought to call a halt. Just drive me home now, and let's say good-bye."

"Not see you again?" he snapped. "You can't expect me to agree to that."

"Oh, we shall see one another," she said with an effort at lightness. "After all, I'm hoping to pick up some commissions for designing jobs when you start selling the apartments in Princess Dock."

Grant turned to face forward, gripping the steering wheel with both hands and staring out through the windshield. After a pause, he said slowly, "I'm afraid you've got to forget all that, Natalie. I'm not going ahead with the Princess Dock project."

"What do you mean . . . you're not going ahead?" She was bewildered.

"Just that. I've been forced to call the whole thing off."

"But why?"

"It's very elementary. The people who were putting up the financing have withdrawn. You'll recall that when you first came to see me I explained that the project wasn't properly off the ground yet. The contract hadn't been inked in, but the backers were very keen. Then they spotted the chance of making a killing in the commodities market, so they diverted their funds to that, which left me high and dry."

"Can't you find someone else to back you?" Natalie asked with concern.

He shook his head. "Cash looking for an investment

is none too plentiful in the present economic climate. I've tried everywhere these past few days. Princess Dock is a first-class project, no question, but it calls for a large injection of capital without immediate returns. No, Natalie, I overstretched myself on this one, and I have no alternative but to pull out."

"But that's terrible for you, Grant."

His lean face twisted into a grim smile. "It's a knock, certainly, but I'll survive it. I've learned how to be a survivor, the hard way. For the present, I'll just have to concentrate on smaller developments and leave the big ones to the large corporations."

"It's such a shame," she said sympathetically. "You had a lot riding on Princess Dock, not just in terms of profit, but prestige-wise as well."

"You too, Natalie. I hate having to kill your hopes."

"Is that why you didn't tell me this afternoon?" she asked, suddenly remembering the incident in Grant's office when he'd been about to say something and checked himself. "Is that why you took me out this evening—to soften the blow?"

"Yes to both questions. I wanted to make sure of you first, to get our relationship on a firmer base. To have told you this news at the office this afternoon might have finished my chances of seeing you again."

"But what I don't understand, Grant, is why you accepted those sketches of mine when you have no use for them now."

"It's hardly *your* fault," he argued, "that the bottom has dropped out of everything."

"Nor yours. So why should *you* be the loser?"

Grant shook his head decisively. "That's not my way of doing things. I stand by my commitments."

On the drive home, Natalie felt acutely uneasy. It was clear to her that, had she not been so persuasive, Grant wouldn't have commissioned her to go ahead with her sketches without having the financial backing of the Princess Dock project securely sewn up by contract.

"About those drawings of mine," she said at length. "You let me do them purely as a favor, didn't you? If I hadn't been so keen, you'd never have suggested that I should work on the project before your cash flow was guaranteed. And now, with things as they are, I don't think it's fair that you should have to pay out for them. So return the portfolio to me, and we'll just forget the whole thing."

"We will not forget it, Natalie." His voice was brusque and he sounded angry. "If you carry out work in good faith, you've every right to be properly recompensed."

"That kind of thinking doesn't make sense," she persisted. "I wouldn't feel comfortable about you paying me for work that you won't be able to use."

"It makes sense to me," he retorted sharply. "That's how it goes in business, Natalie. Are you going to tell me that this is something that's never happened before . . . a job being canceled through no fault of yours? Naturally you expect payment for work done."

She felt her face color up and was grateful for the darkness. But accepting payment from Sir Matthew and Lady Aston for ideas that weren't used was something else entirely. They could easily afford it; besides, the decision not to go ahead was based purely on whim, not forced on them from outside.

"I just thought it would help you," she said lamely.

There was a moment of silence; then Grant said in a gentler voice, "It was a nice gesture, Natalie, and I appreciate it. But I'd prefer to stick to our deal, if you don't mind." Behind the note of gentleness was a hint of steely determination that kept her from saying another word on the subject.

When they arrived back at Chandler's Wharf, Grant

made no move to get out of the car and come in with her. "About tomorrow—" he began.

"No, not tomorrow. I've already told you."

He sighed irritably. "Why are you so determined to punish me?"

"I'm not." It was herself she was punishing, herself she was denying.

"Natalie," he said in a voice that was tight with control, "I want to see you again—soon. If not tomorrow, when? The day after? The one after that?"

She shook her head weakly. "Leave it awhile, Grant."

"How long is 'awhile'?"

She made a vague, uncertain gesture, but she knew that he was intent on pinning her down. "Suppose you call me after the weekend," she suggested.

"Why not before? We could do something together on Sunday."

"No," she stated firmly. It seemed vitally important, somehow, to establish this minimal degree of control over a situation that was threatening to sweep her away. "Call me Monday or Tuesday."

"Monday, then."

He sat quite still, half-turned in his seat to face her. Every last nerve in Natalie's body was intensely aware of him. Though they weren't actually touching, she could sense the rough-smooth texture of his jacket sleeve, almost feel the warm, taut silkiness of his flesh beneath it. Her lips softened in response to the imagined pressure of his lips, and her fingers curled into the remembered crispness of the hair that grew to a point at the nape of his neck. Virility seemed to pulsate from him, enveloping her in sensuous waves of longing for his kiss. Yet when Grant reached out for her, she was electrified into near-hysterical resistance.

"No," she cried, violently twisting away from him. "Please don't!"

"I was only going to kiss you good night, for heaven's sake," he growled, as if trying hard to hold his fraying temper in check. "I'm not a rapist."

"I . . . I don't want you to kiss me. Not now."

"That isn't the message I've been getting," he clipped.

"Then you must have got your lines crossed," she threw back in a vain attempt to take the heat out of the situation.

She heard him draw a quick, ragged breath, and his eyes glinted. But the angry words she expected didn't come. Instead he said in a level tone, "Don't you think I'm entitled to an explanation, Natalie? You and I . . . there's something very special between us, you can't deny that. Yet you keep fighting me as if you were an innocent young girl and I was hell-bent on seducing you. What's it all about, for pity's sake?"

Natalie's heart thudded painfully against her·ribs as she sought frantically for what to say. She couldn't truthfully tell Grant that at this moment the merest touch of his hand on her flesh would ignite flames of longing that would be beyond the power of her will to control. She needed time—time to think calmly about where she was heading, instead of being swept pell-mell into a situation that spelled acute danger to her emotional equilibrium.

"I can't explain," she said unhappily. "It . . . it's all too complicated."

"Is there someone else?" Grant demanded. "Have you got some other commitment you've not told me about?"

"No, there's no one."

"You're sure?" His voice sharpened. "What about Riccardo?"

"Oh, no, there's never been anything between Riccardo and me. We're just neighbors. Good friends."

"Then what is it that's holding you back?" he

persisted. "I don't accept that I've misinterpreted your reactions. Each time I've held you in my arms, I've felt you trembling on the brink of passion. Admit it, Natalie . . . you want me, don't you? You want me every bit as much as I want you."

"Yes, I want you," she said in a shaky whisper.

"Then what's your problem?"

Natalie sighed deeply, knowing that Grant wasn't going to let her wriggle out of an explanation. "I don't imagine it would make much sense to you, even if I could explain. But since my divorce there's been no one . . . and I didn't envisage there ever would be again. I've not felt this way about anyone else I've met, Grant, and . . . I guess I need more time to get a few things straightened out in my mind."

He was silent for a moment; then he reached out his hand and ran his fingertips lightly down her cheek in the tender gesture he had used before. "Okay, Natalie," he said softly. "I don't pretend to understand, but I'll give you the time you need. I won't try to rush you—or not too much, anyway."

She swallowed down a great lump in her throat and tears were very close. Yet she felt a wonderful sense of happiness, of hope. It was as if the ice that had kept her heart frozen all these years was beginning to melt. On a sudden impulse, she leaned forward and gave Grant a feather-light kiss on the cheek.

"Thank you," she murmured. "And thanks too for a lovely evening, Grant. I really enjoyed it."

"That makes two of us," he said, a smile in his voice. "It's promising, wouldn't you say?"

Natalie reached for the door handle and climbed out quickly, while she still had a grip on herself. There was a crack in her voice as she mumbled good night to him.

"Until Monday," Grant said. "I'll call you—first thing."

* * *

It was on Saturday morning that the brilliant idea struck Natalie. In the midst of catching up with neglected household chores she paused, duster in hand, her heart throbbing with excitement. Conviction grew rapidly that this was one of those once-in-a-lifetime opportunities, and it had to be seized. Before she could have timid second thoughts, she went to the phone and tapped out the Astons' London number. If, as was most likely, they were at their house in Hampshire for the weekend, she'd have to leave it until next week.

But she was in luck. Not only was Celia Aston at the Maida Vale apartment, but she answered the phone herself.

"Natalie, how nice to hear from you. I was just feeling a teeny bit sorry for myself at the prospect of a lonely weekend. If you have something you want to discuss, why not come around for lunch? Matthew is out for the day at a golf tournament, and Jodi is off somewhere, so I'm all alone."

This really was too good to be true. Natalie thought a moment, then said, "Actually, Lady Aston, I was wondering if you would have lunch with me. There's something I'd like to show you . . . something I couldn't bring to your apartment."

"You want me to come to your studio instead, you mean? Of course, my dear, I'd be delighted."

"Well, not that either." Oh, dear, it sounded rather a nerve, now that she was saying it. "What I have in mind is to take you to a pub in the East End. It's a rather special place, and . . . well, I'll explain everything when we meet, if you agree."

"I'm intrigued, my dear. I love surprises." Discussing arrangements, Celia Aston insisted on coming to Chandler's Wharf to collect Natalie in her car. "Then you can direct me where to go," she said. "I'm so looking forward to this. You've quite made my day."

Would she still be saying that in a few hours' time? Natalie wondered as she put down the phone. What she was going to suggest required a big leap of imagination on Lady Aston's part, and, much though she liked and respected her client, Natalie wasn't sure that she'd be able to make it.

The Hangman's Noose was an immediate hit with Celia. "How charming!" she exclaimed, glancing around the ancient oak-beamed barroom as they entered. "And how clever of you to find it, Natalie, dear. I shall feel far happier here than I do in the expensive sort of eating places that Matthew insists we need to be seen in these days. Just look at those bottle-glass windowpanes. Genuinely antique, wouldn't you say?"

"Oh, definitely."

When phoning to make a table reservation on the balcony, Natalie hadn't calculated on being recognized by the waitress. She was greeted with a bright, friendly smile.

"The gentleman hasn't been here for lunch since the last time he came with you," the girl said regretfully as she handed them each a menu. "He was getting to be quite a regular. I do hope we haven't lost him."

Cursing the flush that rose to her cheeks, Natalie tried to pass it off with a casual shrug. "I expect he's just been busy elsewhere. I'm sure he'll be back in this area before long."

Celia Aston exclaimed delightedly at the choice of dishes. "It's ages since I tasted steak-and-kidney pie, and boiled-beef-and-carrots used to be Matthew's favorite dish." Her eyes grew misty. "Oh, those were good days, Natalie, when going out for a meal in a pub was the high spot of the week for us. Now, let me see . . . what shall I have?"

Natalie was thankful that her guest's interest in the menu had diverted her attention from the embarrassing subject the waitress had raised, but the moment the girl had departed with their orders, Celia gave her an arch look across the table.

"What was all that about you coming here with an escort?"

"Oh, he was just a business contact," she said, feeling the color flare anew.

"Really?" Celia smiled her disbelief. "You disappoint me, Natalie. I was hoping that you were starting to be sensible, after all."

"I trust that I'm never anything but," Natalie countered with a dismissive laugh.

"I used the wrong word," Celia said, her lips twitching. "You could do with a mite less common sense, my dear, and a little more romance in your outlook. That seems to be a major fault with the modern woman," she added thoughtfully. "A toughness has crept into the feminine character, and romance has flown out of the window."

"It's the age of equality, Lady Aston."

"And I'm all for equality . . . for you younger generation, at least. But it does seem a great pity that so many of the old values have had to go at the same time. Being on equal terms with the man in one's life shouldn't mean that you can't look up to him and respect him too."

"He'd need to be a superman for that." Natalie laughed uneasily.

"Not necessarily," Celia contradicted with heartfelt emphasis. "A man can have many failings, but still be worthy of a woman's admiration and respect." She sighed. "I don't believe Jodi admires or respects anyone in the whole wide world. Certainly not me or her father. She's contemptuous of everything we do or say or think."

"It's just that she's going through a rebellious phase," Natalie said warily. She wished she dared hint that the situation with Jodi might be better if her parents were to stop regarding her as a second-grade substitute for the son they'd lost, and allow the girl to be uniquely herself.

"She is threatening to join some sort of commune now," Celia went on unhappily. "From what I can gather, its aims are quite laudable, conservation and protection of the environment and so on. But from what little I've seen of the people concerned, I'm not very impressed."

Natalie's heart sank. She felt a genuine sympathy for Celia Aston in her concern about Jodi, but just at present she wanted her client in a cheerful frame of mind. "There's a lot of splendid work being done in the conservation field," she ventured. "It's lucky, isn't it, that young people care about what's happening to the environment?"

"Oh, I agree, my dear, and I'm probably being very unfair to Jodi's new friends. But I can't help wishing . . ." Lady Aston gave another sigh, then made a visible effort and smiled at Natalie. "Dear me, you must think I'm a dreadful grouch. But I really am longing to hear why you've brought me here today. Do tell me."

"I will, Lady Aston, as soon as we've finished lunch. Great, here comes our celery soup. It smells good, doesn't it?"

For the next half-hour she managed to keep the conversation flowing along happier lines. But as the minutes ticked by, Natalie's spirits drooped further. The idea which had struck her as so breathtakingly brilliant this morning now seemed crazy. How had she ever imagined it would be possible to convince Lady Aston that this derelict dockland area could be transformed into a fitting site for the city residence of a picky man like Sir Matthew? She would scorn the very idea.

Or worse, Celia's high opinion of her judgment would sink to zero. Still, she'd committed herself too far to duck out now.

To add to her anxiety, Natalie wasn't even certain that she could get the keys to Princess Dock. When they emerged from the pub into bright midday sunshine, replete from a splendid lunch of roast beef and Yorkshire pudding followed by gooseberry pie and thick yellow cream, she led Lady Aston first to the watchman's cottage.

"Hi!" she said brightly when the elderly man opened the door to her knock. "Remember me?"

His age-lined face creased into a smile. "I wouldn't be forgetting a pretty young lady like you. And what can I do for you, miss?"

"I need to take another look around the Princess Dock warehouse," she said, as if it was the most natural thing in the world. "So could I have the keys, please?"

"I don't see why not." He reached behind him to a row of hooks and selected a bunch. "I'll come across with you."

"There's no need," she said quickly. "I'll make sure that I lock up properly and return the keys."

Natalie sighed with relief as he handed them over. The big padlock on the outer gates was stiff, but she managed to open it and ushered her client inside. By this time Celia Aston was very intrigued. Natalie suggested that they perch themselves on one of the big granite bollards, which was warm from the sun, and they sat down facing the warehouse.

"Now, Lady Aston," she began, "I'm going to ask you to use your imagination as you've never done before. Just try to picture the biggest transformation since Cinderella's rags were turned by her fairy godmother into a beautiful ball gown, and the pumpkin into a magnificent coach and horses. Take a good hard look at this derelict warehouse and its surroundings, and try to visualize instead a super-luxury block of apartments surrounded by beautifully laid-out gardens with trees and flowerbeds, and also a swimming pool and tennis courts. That's what it could be like here."

It was a pity, Natalie sighed inwardly, that when delivering her portfolio of sketches to Grant's office she had also handed back the drawing that depicted what the finished site would look like. Knowing how difficult it was for most people to envisage the potential of a conversion, she put everything she had into her word pictures to help Lady Aston see beyond the present shabbiness of the old building, the heaps of rubble in the yard, the slimy green water of the dock basin. Fortunately, perhaps because Lady Aston already trusted her, she was able to get across her own enthusiasm for the project.

"I wonder," Celia mused when at last Natalie ran out of breath. "I wonder what Matthew would think of this. Because of course, Natalie, dear, I realize what you have in mind—that, on this unique site, one of the apartments here would make the ideal London home for us."

"Not just one of the apartments." Natalie smiled, her hopes flaring. "A very special one—the penthouse. Let's go inside and I'll show you."

She led the way up the dark, steep stairs, praying that nothing would kill Lady Aston's interest. But luckily, Celia had come from a tougher background than her present pampered existence. She told Natalie nostalgically that it reminded her of an old derelict factory building in which she and her brother had played as children. When they emerged onto the rooftop, she was still keenly interested.

Once more Natalie launched into her sales pitch, using phrases that she'd rehearsed many times during the past few hours, and this time she had some of her own rough sketches to support what she was saying.

When Natalie pointed out the extensive space for a private roof garden, Lady Aston was captivated.

"Oh, I'd love that," she said wistfully. "Gardening is the thing I miss most when we're in London. Of course, I do have my little conservatory at Maida Vale, but I just live for the times we can slip away to Hampshire and I can get down to some real work in the gardens. Matthew doesn't approve, and keeps asking me what I think we employ staff for. He just can't seem to understand how I feel."

"This penthouse would make the ideal background for a leading financier," Natalie observed, plunging on with her spiel. "It's the sort of place which will get talked about and featured in the media."

Celia nodded vigorously. "I feel very confident that Matthew will like the idea, Natalie, I feel it in my bones. You are so clever, my dear, to have solved our problem. Do you know how soon the development will be completed?"

Natalie swallowed. The moment of truth had arrived. "Well," she confessed, "there's the rub. You see, the developer has run into a problem over finance, and . . . and I was wondering if it might be possible that . . ."

"That Matthew could be persuaded to step in and fill the breach?" queried Celia with a shrewd smile.

"Do you think he would consider it, Lady Aston?"

The older woman was thoughtful. "I really couldn't say, my dear. Matthew has always made it a firm rule never to allow his personal inclinations to color his business judgment. He insists—and I'm sure he's right —that this has to a large measure been the secret of his amazing success. The only way my husband could be persuaded to put money into a project like this would be to convince him that it's a good investment."

"Which I believe it is," Natalie declared. "I'm certain that these apartments will be very much in demand. I was wondering, Lady Aston, if you could broach the subject to Sir Matthew and sound him out. If he's the least bit interested, then obviously he would be supplied with all the information and data he needs to reach a decision."

"I'll talk to him," she agreed with a smile. Then she inquired archly, "And where do you fit into all this, my dear? Is the developer this man friend of yours who's been taking you to lunch at the pub across the road?"

"Yes, but he's not . . . I mean, it's only a business deal between us. I approached him with a view to doing the interior decor of these apartments, and things looked promising. But then he told me the other day that the whole scheme had fallen through. So I thought . . . well, the penthouse here could be turned into a marvelous London home for you and Sir Matthew. And if your husband liked the idea, he might consider the Princess Dock project as a possible investment."

Celia Aston gave an indulgent little laugh. "Does the man in question know that you're approaching me, Natalie? Was it perhaps his suggestion?"

"Oh, no!" she said emphatically. "It was entirely my idea. You must believe that. Grant would never make a back-door approach."

"Grant, eh? And what is his other name, might I inquire?"

"It's Kilmartin—as I see you've already guessed." Natalie felt her cheeks grow warm again. "Yes, Lady Aston, he's the man behind the shopping-arcade development opposite your present home."

Celia chuckled, looking delighted. "I see. Well, that's all to the good, isn't it? Matthew has been most impressed with the businesslike way in which that particular development has been handled. So I'll be happy to pass on to him the name of this young man—for whom you feel nothing but a strictly professional interest, Natalie, dear—and I'll tell him about

your penthouse idea. But of course," she added warningly, "I can promise nothing."

For the remainder of the weekend Natalie stayed
home, making a pretense of working. Her spirits kept
fluctuating wildly between high peaks of hope and
troughs of despair—because, surely, her crazy idea
couldn't possibly work out.

Monday brought the added complication that Grant
would be calling to fix a date. She'd have to stall him.
How could she meet him face to face and not blurt out
what she'd done?

During the morning and afternoon the phone rang
several times. Always her heart thudded painfully as
she snatched up the receiver, and always she had the
dismal anticlimax of its being just another business call.
Except once, when a man she'd dated a couple of times
recently, a lawyer specializing in international trade
agreements, called to say that he was back now from
the legal symposium which had taken him to Switzer-
land for the past couple of weeks, and would she have
dinner with him. Natalie found an excuse for each of
the three evenings he suggested and he hung up,
sounding hurt. She doubted that she'd hear from him
again, but the thought caused scarcely a riffle in her
mind.

By late Monday evening she was in a bad state of
nerves. What had gone wrong? So much for Grant's
impatient eagerness to see her again! She rechecked
her answering machine to make sure he hadn't left a
message when she was out, though the farthest she'd
been all day was to post a letter.

Tuesday was even worse than Monday, if that were
possible. It was a heavily overcast day, hot and humid
for early May and with the threat of thunder in the air,
which didn't help matters. In the early evening Natalie
took a cooling shower, then pulled on fawn cotton

shorts and a yellow top that left her midriff bare. She made herself a simple salad of a few lettuce leaves with some walnuts and crumbled blue cheese, and took it out to her patio, which overlooked the canal at the rear of her studio. Tucked away out here, she couldn't hear cars driving into the courtyard. A loud rapping on her front door brought her leaping to her feet in startled awareness.

It was Grant—she knew that instinctively. And by the sound of it, he was in a towering rage.

Chapter Five

"You took your time," Grant rasped when she'd gathered her courage to open the door to him.

"I'm sorry," she stammered. "I was—"

"You've cause to be sorry, Natalie. But I doubt if you really are." He thrust past her into the studio. "What the devil did you think you were up to, poking your nose into something that's none of your business?"

Natalie stared at him in dismay, wishing she could see something other than black fury in the way he was looking at her. "Is it to do with the Princess Dock and Sir Matthew Aston?"

"What else?" he barked. "How in the hell d'you imagine I feel, having you go behind my back and cook up a deal like this?"

"I was trying to help you," she protested miserably.

"Help yourself, you mean! You saw the chance of a nice fat designing contract, and you grabbed it with both hands. Never mind the spot you put me on."

"That's not true!" she cried, shocked. "I wasn't thinking of myself."

"No?" Grant's voice was thick with sarcasm. "It never once crossed your mind, I suppose, that if the Princess Dock scheme could be kept alive, you'd come out a winner?"

Natalie flushed a bright pink. However much she protested the truth—that the advantage to herself had been such a minimal factor that it hardly came into the picture—she could never expect Grant to believe her, not in his present mood.

"I did it *mainly* for your sake," she insisted with all the spirit she could dredge up. "It just seemed a crying shame that you were having to jettison a splendid development like that because your backers had withdrawn. I won't make out I didn't also realize that I would stand to gain, too, if the project could be saved."

"If it depended on me," Grant stated, his eyes sparking with fury, "you wouldn't stand to gain the thinnest slice of the action. But you've fixed it for yourself to cut off a nice fat wedge."

Natalie was bewildered. "What are you talking about, Grant?"

"I'm talking about the fact that Mrs. Natalie Kent has been named as official design consultant for the Princess Dock development. It's a prerequisite laid down by our generous benefactor, Sir Matthew Aston."

"But that can't be true . . ." Natalie protested, then trailed off as she realized it was only too possible. Here was a sign of Lady Aston's kind-natured manipulating. The Princess Dock project would be viewed by Sir Matthew purely as a business proposition to be backed with his capital resources if it looked a sound, profitable scheme, or left well alone if not. But to slip in a condition that Natalie Kent should be the design consultant would be a neat way of indulging his wife's fancy without in any way deviating from his strict, self-imposed rule in business deals.

Without doubt, it would give a terrific boost to her standing as a designer—far more than she'd ever hoped to gain in prestige when she first approached Grant. But faced with his hostility, she felt no thrill of excitement. If she accepted this wonderful offer it would only make Grant feel even more bitter toward her than he did now—aside from the fact that she could hardly hope to turn out inspired designs if she and the developer were at dagger point.

Swiftly on the heels of this bleak thought came a feeling of anger that Grant should be so ungrateful. Couldn't he see that she'd gone out on a limb for his sake? He might at least manage to mutter a thank-you.

"I believe," he said witheringly, "it's on the tip of your tongue to deny any wish to be involved in the project. Go ahead. You might as well add blatant lying to your outrageous interference."

She took a deep, shuddering breath and glared back at him. "You don't have to worry, Grant, I absolve you from any need to employ me as design consultant."

Grant swung away impatiently and strode to the open French windows, standing with his back to her. "How easy to make that self-sacrificing gesture," he ground out sarcastically. "Because you know damn well that it's a non-starter. Either I do the development with you stringing along, or I don't do the development. It's as elementary as that."

"Nobody can force me to work with you," Natalie flared rebelliously. "Not if I say I don't want to."

"And nobody can *force* Sir Matthew to release the necessary funds, if *he* says he doesn't want to." Grant's whole frame stiffened and she saw the taut anger in every muscle. "It depends on you, Natalie, whether or not my Princess Dock scheme goes ahead. Only, I warn you, don't expect me to go down on hands and knees and beg for your kind cooperation. To hell with that! I'd rather go bankrupt and lose everything I've ever worked for."

"If you feel so strongly about working with me," she said in a cold, hostile voice, "there's nothing to stop you refusing Sir Matthew's offer. Then you'd be back to square one, looking for someone to put up the cash."

Grant spun around and threw her a look of chilling

hatred. "You ought to know enough about the way things work in business to realize that the outcome would be totally different. Grant Kilmartin would be tagged a difficult man to work with, and I'd find myself unable to raise finance for future projects. No, Natalie, thanks to your meddling I'll have to swallow my pride and accept Sir Matthew Aston and his intolerable stipulation about employing you."

"Charming!" she said grittily. "I try to give you a helping hand, and all you can do in return is insult me."

"I prefer to do without 'helping hands.'"

"Okay, I'll remember that," she said in a choked voice. "I won't stick my neck out again for your sake, Grant. In fact," she added, "I'll take care to keep well out of your way in future."

"Considerate of you." He sneered. "But it's hardly going to be possible, is it? We shall be falling over one another the whole time."

"There's no reason why things shouldn't work out." She was forcing a note of brightness, to make the incredible sound possible. "It's all to the good that our relationship won't be complicated by a personal angle. We're two intelligent people, Grant, and as long as we limit ourselves to business, we should be able to coexist."

He stared at her moodily for a long moment, his gaze sweeping over her slender body, and for the first time Natalie became aware of her scant clothing. She wanted to retreat to her bedroom to find something that would cover her better, but that would hand Grant a sort of victory. She could just picture the gleam of sardonic amusement in his eyes. So she boldly stood her ground and outstared him.

"I think you'd better leave now," she said icily.

"Leave?" He sounded surprised.

"There's no point in your staying any longer, is there? You've said what you came to say to me—in telling language. Your view of the situation couldn't be more crystal clear. You don't have to worry, Grant, you'll get my cooperation. But we must try to eradicate the need for us to meet. I'll deal with the Kilmartin Development Corporation via members of your staff, not via you. Okay?"

"Suits me fine," he clipped.

They stood facing one another, their eyes incandescent with anger. In the throbbing silence the tension mounted, reaching a height that was dangerously close to flashpoint. Natalie felt the prickle of tears behind her eyes, and fought to keep them in check. How gratified he would be to have made her cry! And anyway, what would she be crying for? With Grant's change of feeling toward her she had lost nothing of real value, while she had gained something infinitely precious. In a couple of years from now her reputation would have soared to a dizzy peak. The name Natalie Kent would count among the elite of British designers. Her golden opportunity was right here; the world was laid at her feet.

So why did she have this feeling of blank despair?

"I'll see that you're notified as soon as things are sewn up with Sir Matthew Aston," Grant said in a terse voice.

"Thank you." This, she thought despondently, would have to be the tone of their relationship whenever they did chance to meet up. A cold, freezing politeness that held anger at bay.

"I'll leave you to get on with your evening," he muttered.

"Yes," she said levelly, "I'd appreciate that. I have a number of things I want to get done." She plunged on in an effort to relax the tension she could feel building up again. "I'll look forward to hearing from you in due course . . . or rather, from your secretary."

Grant nodded, but still made no move to leave. As

she went past him to open the door, he put out a hand and touched her arm. "Natalie, I—"

She tore herself away as if his fingertips would scorch her. She had to fight to control the trembling which shook her whole body. Her legs suddenly felt numb and she dared not take another step.

"Just go, will you?" she said huskily. "Let yourself out."

Another tension-filled pause, then Grant shrugged, his eyes hardening to chips of granite. "Good night, then."

"Good night."

As he reached the door, a curious kind of cry escaped her lips, halfway to being a sob. Grant looked back swiftly. "What were you going to say, Natalie?"

She improvised wildly, to cover up her shameful cry from the heart. "Er . . . how soon do you expect to get the go-ahead from Sir Matthew?"

"At the moment, he has his team of experts making a feasibility study of the Princess Dock scheme. I haven't a doubt that he'll get a thumbs-up from them, and he isn't a man to hang about. So I imagine that we'll know in a few days."

"I see."

Natalie stood where she was, still trembling, until long after she heard Grant drive away. Amid the confused tangle of her emotions, a stray thought came to her as a lifeline to grasp. One thing she ought to do now was call Celia Aston. Had she foreseen Grant's angry reaction, of course, she'd never have broached the subject of Sir Matthew putting up the money for Princess Dock, but as things stood, a proper display of gratitude was called for.

"I wanted to say thank you, Lady Aston," she said when she got through. "It looks as if the Princess Dock scheme is going ahead, thanks to Sir Matthew."

"It's we who should be thanking you, my dear. The penthouse there will be quite perfect as our London home. Matthew entirely agrees with me that it has all the right elements for someone in his position." Despite her friendliness, Celia wasn't her usual cheerful self. There was a note in her voice that suggested she had something on her mind.

"I hope I'm not calling at an inconvenient time," Natalie said uncomfortably.

"Not at all, my dear, we've finished dinner."

"You sound a little upset, though. Is something wrong?"

"It's nothing of consequence," Celia said dismissively. "Tell me, how are things progressing between you and that nice young man of yours, Mr. Kilmartin? He must be delighted with you for being so clever when he was facing difficulties."

"Grant Kilmartin is not my young man, Lady Aston. As I told you the other day, we're just business associates. That applies even more so now," she added before she could stop herself.

Once again Celia Aston jumped to a shrewd conclusion. "He's not sulking because you spoke up on his behalf? Isn't that just like a man? But I'm sure he'll soon come round and realize how unfair he's being, dear."

"Oh, but things suit me fine the way they are," Natalie insisted, trying to inject conviction into her voice. "He's going to benefit, and so am I. It was terribly good of you to put in a word for me with your husband and get him to have me named the design consultant. A job on the scale of the Princess Dock conversion will really establish me in my career."

"I'm only too delighted to have been able to help, Natalie. You're a very talented young woman, and you've worked hard. You deserve every success. But I do beg you, my dear, not to place too much importance on building your career . . . not to the exclusion of even more important aspects of life."

Desperate to switch the subject, Natalie blurted out, "How are things with Jodi, Lady Aston?"

Celia sighed. "Not good at all, I'm afraid. We had a most distressing scene earlier this evening, which is why I sounded upset. I'm really at my wits' end with her."

Natalie didn't know what to say. She fell back on the sort of soothing platitudes about its being a difficult age that Jodi was going through.

"But most girls," Celia bemoaned, "don't take a positive pleasure in angering their parents. I certainly didn't at that age, and I'm quite sure you didn't, either."

"I don't suppose I was any better than average," Natalie said candidly. "I know that after my parents were both killed, when I was at college, I wished I'd been more thoughtful of them."

"Oh, my dear, I didn't realize that you had lost your parents so young. How tragic for you. And then all the distress of an unhappy marriage. Clearly you've faced life with great courage and determination. I admire you immensely, Natalie, which is why I'm so anxious that you shouldn't let the experience of a broken marriage make you hard and uncaring. Those qualities are not natural in a woman, my dear. Men are so much better than we are at being single-mindedly dedicated to their careers."

"Men have had things their own way for too long," Natalie pointed out firmly. "It's more than time we women showed them that we're just as capable of making our mark in the world as they are."

"I suppose you're right," Celia conceded. "Up to a point. Is that what Jodi is trying to do, do you think— make her mark in the world?"

"In a sense, I suppose. She's feeling her way."

There was another heavy sigh at the end of the line.

"All I can say is, it's a pity that life has to be such a joyless business. Surely at seventeen it should be full of happiness and laughter, as it was for our dear son, Keith. But I'm being tactless again, Natalie, dear. There can't have been much fun and laughter in your life. Still, it's not too late—if you'll only bear in mind that—"

Seeing danger looming ahead once more, Natalie cut in hastily, "I mustn't keep you any longer, Lady Aston. I just felt I had to say thank you for what you've done to help me."

"Perhaps, Natalie, dear," came the thoughtful reply, "there'll be something more I can do for you. We shall have to see."

As the days dragged by, Natalie struggled to get into a calm enough state of mind to do good creative work. She had plenty of commissions on hand: a semi-basement flat in a large Victorian house in Islington, a super-luxury bathroom for the lead singer of a pop group, and the members' lounge for an offbeat theater club at Notting Hill Gate. Perhaps, she thought wryly, it was a pity that none of these jobs demanded her urgent attention. As it was, time and again she caught herself glancing up from her drawing board and staring blankly into space, staring at the image of Grant's face, his jaw set rock-hard, his dark eyes ablaze with anger.

Until her approach to Lady Aston, until what he'd chosen to call her meddling in his business, Grant had found her attractive, desirable, and he'd wanted to make love to her. Might it not have been better, she found herself wondering, not to have fought so hard against her own insidious longing? If they were lovers now, she thought, her breath catching in her throat, she would be partway along the road to getting Grant

Kilmartin out of her system. Hadn't he said himself, answering a quip of hers, that buildings were made to last, whereas love affairs were not? And of course he was right. A love affair that was based on nothing more than a sexual attraction would flare brightly for a short time and soon burn itself out. She wasn't an emotional innocent; she'd been married and she knew her way around. Up until now, since her divorce, she'd steered clear of any involvement with a man in favor of concentrating on her career. But if absorption with a particular man reached a point where it actually endangered your career, wasn't it crazy to deny yourself the sexual gratification he offered?

It was too late, though, to be thinking like that. Grant was furious with her, and from now on he wanted to see no more of her than was unavoidable . . . while she herself was left with the bitter knowledge that she would go on being tormented by dreams of the blissful hours they could have shared in one another's arms.

On Saturday morning, just as she was finishing her meager breakfast, Riccardo called round in great excitement.

"*Cara,* you are the very first one I tell." Stepping inside, he grabbed her by the waist and twirled her around gaily. "I have wonderful news. Maria and I—we have settled the day at last."

"That's really great," Natalie exclaimed. "But how have you been able to fix things, Riccardo? What about her father's café? Will Maria still have to work there when you're married?"

"No, no, everything is beautifully arranged. Her Aunt Anna—Signore Gaspari's sister—she is coming from Italy to take Maria's place. So Maria is free at last to be my wife, and we can return to Napoli. I am so happy, I cannot tell you, Natalie."

"And I'm happy for you, Riccardo, for you both."

"You will celebrate with Maria and me, yes? Tonight, at the café? At eleven o'clock, when it closes, we will have a big party for our friends. I shall go now and tell Diane and the others. Everyone is invited."

As he bounded off to spread his glad tidings, Natalie smiled after him wistfully. Lucky Maria, to be loved so devotedly and so patiently by a thoroughly nice guy like Riccardo.

That evening at the Café Napoli, the chairs and tables had been pushed to one side and the room was decorated with colored lights and a mass of flowers. When she and Diane arrived together after the brief walk from Chandler's Wharf, the party was already in full swing. The two girls were greeted by the plump, genial Signore Gaspari, and then by the happy couple. Maria was a darkly pretty girl with large, friendly black eyes and a sensuous mouth. She accepted their warm congratulations with a blissful smile. Riccardo, one arm possessively around her waist, plied them with ruby-red Chianti from a giant two-liter flask, and told them to help themselves from the piled-up buffet of Italian delicacies which occupied a group of tables that had been pushed together. The smell was mouth-watering, and they fell upon the food avidly.

A couple of hours later, Diane was in a somberly reflective mood. Giving a heavy sigh, she grumbled to Natalie, "Just look at Riccardo and Maria . . . they're disgustingly happy. Some people have all the luck."

"You don't begrudge them, Di?"

"Who, me? I just wish I could have a tiny share of such luck myself."

Natalie laughed. "You seem to do all right. What about your current boyfriend . . . Frank, isn't it? You were raving about him the other day."

"Oh, Frank's okay. Only he's like all the other guys I've ever met, out for a good time and no ties." She stared moodily at her half-empty glass and took another gulp.

"Could be," Natalie suggested, "that you'd do better to fix your sights on a different sort of man, Di. The steadier type, who's looking for something more permanent."

"What would you know about it?" Diane challenged. "You haven't had much success in the 'till-death' stakes, have you? Seems to me you've not had much success with men, period. If you want my opinion, Natalie, you just don't know how to handle them. You blow all your chances. What about Grant Kilmartin? That situation was looking nicely promising, but I've not seen him around Chandler's Wharf this past week or two."

Natalie bristled. "I wish you'd get it into your skull, Di, there was never anything going between Grant Kilmartin and me."

"More fool you, then! The guy showed real interest in you, and he only needed a modicum of encouragement. Any man worth having isn't going to stand for repeated brush-offs. They soon get bored and look for a pasture where the grass is less thistly."

"It sounds to me," Natalie said with a dismissive laugh, "as if you've been drinking too much of Signore Gaspari's good vino. You'd better go easy, or I'll have to carry you home."

Diane grinned at her amiably. "Don't worry, I haven't had too much to drink. Just enough to tell you straight out what I think."

"You do that anyway," Natalie countered, "even when you're as sober as a judge."

"Well, you ought to listen to the voice of hard-won experience."

Natalie decided it was time to change the subject.

"Hey, we're becoming a couple of wet rags. This is supposed to be a celebration."

A couple of evenings later, when Natalie was washing up her supper dishes, there was a knock at the front door. She opened it to find Grant standing there.

"You've gone and done it again, haven't you?" he blazed.

Shocked and stunned, Natalie was unable to find her voice. She just stared at him mutely, a hand to the pulse that beat in her throat.

"You and I had better have a clear understanding," he raged on, thrusting past her into the studio as before. "This is the last time I'll stand for you meddling in my business. Any more of your tricks, and to hell with the consequences. I won't be pushed around."

"What . . . what are you talking about?" she whispered huskily.

"As if you didn't know. Exactly what are you trying to pull, Natalie? Are you aiming to be an equal partner with me in the Princess Dock development? Because if so, then I'll disabuse you here and now. I intend to run this project *my* way, and you'll be nothing more than the interior-design consultant, answerable to *me*. Got that?"

"Of course," she stammered. "I never expected anything else."

"So why are you scheming your way right up front? This invitation from Sir Matthew Aston for the two of us to spend next weekend at Hartwell Manor—"

Natalie gasped in astonishment. "It's news to me."

"Don't pull that innocent act," he grated. "You worked on Lady Aston to get us both invited to their place. You're much too close to that woman, Natalie."

"Lady Aston is a *client* of mine," she protested. "I admit that we're on friendly terms, but as for—"

"You told me yourself," Grant interrupted in a

sarcastic tone, "that you find it difficult to keep work
relationships and personal relationships in separate
boxes—or had you forgotten? You don't fool me,
Natalie. It's glaringly obvious that you're using
your leverage with her ladyship to grab the most you
can."

She felt color rise to her face. This invitation might
have been issued by Sir Matthew, but she couldn't
doubt that his wife was behind it. And Natalie could
guess why: to push her and Grant together. Lady
Aston, despite her husband's autocratic chauvinism,
was a happily married woman, and like all happily
married women, she was a deep-eyed romantic at
heart. Not content with constantly urging Natalie to
find herself a Mr. Right, she was now trying to manipu-
late things. Natalie shuddered with dismay at the
recollection of Celia Aston's parting words on the
phone the last time they'd spoken. *Perhaps, Natalie,
dear, there'll be something more I can do for you. We
shall have to see.*

Natalie forced herself to meet Grant's accusing gaze,
though inwardly she was quaking. "Whatever brought
about that invitation to Hartwell Manor, it was none of
my seeking. I swear it, Grant."

"Easy to swear," he grated. "Impossible to prove."

"I'll prove it," she flashed back, "by not going."

"On what grounds?" His eyes were stony. "This sort
of invitation is like a royal command. You can't refuse it
on the pretext of a prior engagement."

A moment's thought was enough for Natalie to
realize that she could never hope to make Lady Aston
understand the true, complex nature of her relationship
with Grant without going into details that were far too
embarrassing to be recounted.

"I . . . I could say that I've got flu or something,"
she suggested unhappily.

The scorn in his voice cracked at her like a whip. "Do

you always find it easy to lie your way out of difficulties, Natalie?"

"I was only trying to suggest a tactful solution."

"Knowing that I wouldn't agree," he snapped.

"Why not? You say you don't want me to go with you to Hartwell Manor, yet when I offer a sensible out, you won't listen."

"Your 'sensible out' is the sort of story cooked up by some kid typist who hasn't the guts to say straight out that she wants some time off. I won't have it."

Natalie refused to admit defeat. "I wasn't asking *you* to make an excuse, Grant. I'd be the one."

"It would still be my responsibility. You're an associate of mine now, whether I like it or not—which I don't."

"But I'm not one of your kid typists," Natalie said coldly. "So don't think you can treat me like one."

In his anger, she thought with a catch of breath, Grant looked magnificent. His head thrown proudly back, his eyes glinting sparks, he seemed to be daring her to provoke him just once more. What if she did? she wondered defiantly. He looked capable of grabbing hold of her and shaking her into submission. She took a step backward, because his very nearness represented a hazard. Grant's touch, the first contact of those whipcord fingers, would sweep away her strength and determination to stand up to him.

If Grant had noticed her shrinking away from him, he gave no sign of it. "About the weekend," he said in a terse, abrupt voice, as if winding up a discussion he found infinitely distasteful. "I'll pick you up at five-thirty on Friday. We're expected in good time for dinner at eight."

"I'd prefer to get there under my own steam," Natalie threw back.

"Now you're being stupidly petty," he said accusingly. "In any case, the drive to Hampshire will give us a chance to decide on our strategy."

The thought of spending an hour or more with Grant in the close confinement of his car was awesome. But there was no way of dodging it. The pit she had dug for herself by first approaching Lady Aston about the Princess Dock project seemed to be growing deeper and deeper.

Suppose she had succumbed to Grant and the two of them *were* lovers? Natalie reflected with a shiver after he had slammed out. Would he still be furious with her for "meddling"? She sank into an armchair and hugged her hands to her bare arms as if she were cold. She was long past the stage of pretending with herself. Her body felt an intense sensual thirst that had been awakened by Grant, a deep, unfulfilled longing that wouldn't easily be quenched. She had been crazy not to seize the chance of letting him make love to her while the possibility still existed. But now it was clear that he had lost all interest in her as a lover. He was only keeping the contact with her alive because it was necessary to him from a business standpoint.

How was she ever going to survive this coming weekend, being paired with Grant in the informal atmosphere of a house party? Lady Aston, she felt sure, would grasp every opportunity to push them together into intimate situations. The weekend loomed like a dark, threatening cloud; yet, paradoxically, Natalie found herself looking forward to it. She would rather be in Grant's company even in his present mood of bitter anger toward her, she realized to her dismay and humiliation, than not be with him at all.

Chapter Six

*H*ow enchanting!" Natalie cried out involuntarily as Grant swung his dark blue Alfa Romeo through the tall wrought-iron gates and Hartwell Manor came into view at the end of its long, curving driveway, bathed now in the mellow glow of evening sunshine.

"It's an architectural gem," he agreed affably.

The drive down to Hampshire from London had been a torture to Natalie, with long, emotion-charged silences punctuated by cool exchanges about what the weekend ahead might achieve. Grant demanded to know if she was wised-up and ready to expound her ideas about the interior decor of Princess Dock to Sir Matthew and Lady Aston—or any of their guests who might show interest—and she assured him stiffly that she knew her own area every bit as well as he knew his.

However, this first glimpse of the grand mansion seemed to unfreeze Grant. Set in rolling parkland and built foursquare of weathered red brick and tawny stonework, a central pediment carved with elaborate scrolls and curlicues, it presented a picture of gracious solidity, a fitting residence for landed gentry through centuries of checkered history. It was on record, Lady Aston had once told Natalie, that several monarchs had honored Hartwell Manor with royal visits, while at other periods antiroyalist plots were said to have been hatched there. And now it belonged to a man who had risen from humblest origins to become one of the wealthiest men in all England.

Grant drew up the car before a wide apron of steps that was flanked by two Grecian urns of carved white marble. A white-jacketed manservant came running down the steps to take the car keys from Grant, and they mounted together to where a graver black-clad figure awaited them. It was the first time ever, Natalie thought with a thrill, that she'd encountered a real-life butler. Greeted deferentially, they were passed over to a young maidservant who escorted them up the grand stairway to their bedrooms, Grant's just along the corridor from hers. Her luggage, she found, had miraculously arrived ahead of her.

"Will that be all, madam?" asked the maid before withdrawing. "Dinner is in forty-five minutes. Cocktails will be served in the library when you care to go down."

Left alone, Natalie studied the room. The designer had known what he was about; she had to grant him that, even if his handling of Lady Aston had been short on tact. The decor was impeccable, with nothing strident or overstated. It was a harmony of muted color, from the delicate ivory and eggshell-blue of the molded plaster ceiling to the deeper hyacinth blue of the Aubusson carpet. The walls were hung with silk flock in a medallion design of magnolia and pale gold, while the bedcover, chairs and window draperies were richly elegant in a soft shade of mulberry taffeta. The long windows, opening to a balcony, looked over the grounds to the tree-clad greenness of rural meadowland. Beyond, a line of gently rounded hills rose as a backcloth in the distance.

With an appreciative sigh, Natalie began unpacking her things. Then she showered and slipped into the dress she'd brought to wear this evening—a pale apricot crêpe-de-chine, with tiny pleats that flared softly around her slim legs as she walked. If only, she thought wistfully as she dabbed perfume behind her ears and at her wrists, this weekend were a less tension-fraught occasion, it would be fun to wallow in sheer luxury for once.

A tap at her door brought the heart-clenching fear that it was Grant. But to her relief it turned out to be Celia Aston.

"I just wanted to make sure that you're comfortable, my dear. How pretty you look in that dress."

"Thank you, Lady Aston. This is a beautiful room, and a beautiful house altogether. It was very kind of you to invite me . . . us."

Her hostess pursed her lips in a smile. "I thought it might help a little. How are things between you two—all smoothed over now?"

"I'm afraid you have quite the wrong idea," Natalie protested, knowing that it was in vain. "There really isn't anything between us, except for business."

"In which case," said Celia, her smile switching to archness, "this weekend will give you a chance to get to know one another better. Now, my dear, if you're quite ready, shall we go down together?"

On the way down, Natalie had more chance to take note of her surroundings than when coming up with Grant. The wide stairway curved elegantly around the entrance hall, with a massive glass lantern suspended on thirty feet of bronze chain from the domed ceiling high overhead. Paintings worthy of any art gallery graced the walls, portraits in oils of ladies and gentlemen from past ages. "I'm afraid that we can't claim them as genuine ancestors," Lady Aston said with a little laugh. "We inherited them with the house, so to speak."

Evening sunlight flooding in through two tall French windows dazzled Natalie's eyes as they entered the drawing room, where clusters of people stood chatting, drinks in hand. She looked around for Grant but he wasn't there. Moments later he appeared from the terrace in the company of a tall, thin gray-haired man who was presumably their host.

"Matthew, dearest, come and meet Mrs. Kent," Celia called.

Sir Matthew came forward and took her hand, while his pale gray eyes, though friendly and welcoming, assessed her shrewdly. "So you're the clever young woman who's going to make us a very special home at Princess Dock—eh?"

"I hope so, Sir Matthew." Natalie was burningly aware of Grant's gaze on her, though she avoided looking in his direction. She was on trial with him, she knew; he was just waiting for her to wrong-foot. "What I aim to do," she added brightly, "is to create the perfect background for you and Lady Aston in the penthouse there . . . a home of style and elegance, and yet with a sufficiently informal atmosphere for you to feel completely relaxed."

"Capital!" he said, nodding approval. "And I don't doubt that you'll be able to manage it, my dear, to judge from the way your praises have been sung."

By Grant? she wondered with a catch of breath, and couldn't help stealing a quick glance at him. He looked straight back at her stonily, his dark eyes denying any such possibility.

"My wife thinks the world of you," Sir Matthew went on. "You have a real champion in Lady Aston, you know, Mrs. Kent."

But not in Grant, she thought bitterly. In his present mood he wouldn't have a solitary good word to say for her. Her services had been demanded as a prerequisite of Sir Matthew's financial backing, but it would choke Grant to pretend that he liked the idea.

The room where they dined was a glory of green and

gold, with white pilasters soaring to carved Corinthian capitals. Twenty people sat around the long table, which gleamed with white napery, fine bone china, and glittering silver and glass. The other guests seemed mostly to be connected with Sir Matthew in some business capacity—a banker, a stockbroker, his financial adviser and the managing director of a group of his subsidiary companies, all here with their wives.

Conscious of Grant's sardonic gaze from across the table, Natalie tried to keep up a vivacious conversation with the man on her right, though it was tough going. Tom Skinner, it had emerged during the introductions, was Lady Aston's younger brother. From his air of diffidence, Natalie guessed that his executive job at Aston Financial Holdings had been manufactured for him. She felt quite sorry for the man, obliged to mold himself to a way of life that was totally alien to his temperament—in rather the same way as his sister. Her sympathy was underscored by the flamboyant behavior of Tom's wife, Blanche, seated beside Grant, a woman who dressed expensively and talked in a loud, carrying voice.

"Do tell me, Mr. Kilmartin," she gushed, "what it is exactly that a property developer *does.*"

"That depends on the man," Grant replied evenly. "Some developers are only interested in building from scratch on virgin land, or if it's an old site, they raze to the ground first. For myself, I concentrate on those areas—or in some cases specific buildings—which have deteriorated for one reason or other. I try to find a new use for them that's applicable to the modern world."

"How very laudable." She laughed. "And profitable, too, no doubt?"

"But of course," he responded, laughing back at her. "There's no sense going into business unless it's to make money."

"How right you are." She dropped her voice so that it became inaudible to Natalie. Blanche Skinner, Natalie pondered sourly, was no doubt just Grant's type; another of the enameled, sexy blondes who were lookalikes of his ex-wife. From the blatant way she was flirting with him it seemed clear that he'd have no trouble adding her to his score of conquests. Natalie laid down her fork, suddenly finding herself choked by the wafer-thin smoked salmon.

"Mrs. Kent would be the one to answer that," she heard Grant say suddenly. "What about it, Natalie?"

She jerked herself out of her brooding. "I'm sorry, I didn't . . ."

"Mrs. Skinner just said that while she can appreciate the need for the imaginative conversion of old buildings, she considers that a good deal of interior decor is shockingly overdone. 'Chichi' was the word she used." His expression was blandly inquiring. "I take it that you wouldn't agree with her?"

Did Grant imagine he was throwing her to the wolves? Raising her chin, Natalie met his gaze coldly. "You're mistaken, then, Grant. I entirely accept that a great deal of modern decor is in bad taste."

She must have spoken up louder than she'd intended. The remark had the effect of stilling other conversations around the table; all eyes were turned in her direction. Much embarrassed, Natalie continued defiantly, "I'd even go so far as to say that *most* modern interior decor is in bad taste—or overdone, or chichi, or just plain awful. All of which is an argument in favor of my profession."

"*Against* it, you mean," Blanche drawled, looking faintly bewildered.

"Did it sound that way to you?" Natalie asked sweetly. She glanced around the table with a pasted-on smile. "No one here, I'm sure, would consider using an

unqualified person in the capacity of doctor, or lawyer
. . . or even plumber. People accept the need for
calling on someone who knows what he's about. But
when it comes to interior decor, it's so often thought
that one only has to assemble a few items of furniture,
then choose the wallpaper and a carpet and the curtain
fabric and some cushions, and it's blithely expected that
the result will look okay. Only, usually, the result is
sheer disaster—there's no style, no overall theme, the
colors and patterns fight, and the essential quality of
restraint is totally lacking. Some people—I wouldn't
deny it for a moment—have a natural flair for harmony;
such people, when doing-it-for-themselves in their own
homes, can achieve a happy effect. Bully for them. But
if you happen to own a house or other piece of property
that is worthy of the best—and you can afford the
best—then isn't it foolhardy not to employ the services
of someone with the right expertise?"

"Like you, I suppose?" Blanche interjected, a sneer
curling her lower lip.

"Like me," Natalie agreed calmly. "Or like the
interior designer who did this house for Sir Matthew
and Lady Aston. It's the creation of a true genius.
There's a subtle blending of traditional features discreetly augmented by the use of modern materials and
techniques. The effect is superb. My guess is that
Hartwell Manor looks better now than it has ever done
in all its long history."

From their places at either end of the long table,
Lady Aston smiled contentedly while her husband
looked hugely gratified. "That's put you in your place,
Blanche!" He chuckled, the slight edge to his tone
suggesting to Natalie that he had no great liking for the
woman his brother-in-law had married.

After dinner everyone adjourned to the drawing
room again for coffee. Several of the men went off with

Sir Matthew to play billiards, and a couple of tables were set up for bridge fours. A hired pianist played tunes from musical shows on the magnificent grand piano. Natalie strolled to the farther end of the room and stood admiring a bronze-and-ormolu console table on which rested a matching pair of fine Sèvres vases in the delicate rose color created specially for Madame de Pompadour, the pampered mistress of the French emperor Louis the Fifteenth.

"You've clawed your way into Sir Matthew's good books, haven't you?" Grant's sneering voice came from right behind her. "You already had his wife cheerleading for you, and now the great man himself is joining in. I've got to hand it to you, Natalie, you're a real ball of fire."

She wheeled around on him accusingly. "Why did you have to say what you did at dinner, Grant? If we're going to have to work together, it's best that we don't snipe at one another in public."

"Was I sniping?"

"You expected me to be totally crushed by your quoting Blanche Skinner's catty remark."

"If I expected that," he said softly, his lips twitching in amusement, "I'd seriously underestimated you, hadn't I? You came out of your corner fighting, Natalie, and made mincemeat of her."

"I wasn't going to let myself be beaten by a person like Blanche," she said vehemently. "Or by you!"

Grant gave her an odd look that she couldn't interpret. "I'd better watch out. The way you can twist a big shot like our host around your little finger proves that you're a dangerous antagonist."

"We shouldn't be thinking of ourselves as antagonists at all," Natalie muttered crossly. She'd kept her voice discreetly low, but even so she caught a swift, surprised glance from Lady Aston, who was at one of the bridge tables. "We're drawing attention," she added warningly.

"Then let's go outside," he suggested.

"No, thanks."

"Actually, it would be a prudent move on our part."

"Prudent?"

"That's what I said. It's clear that Lady Aston harbors romantic notions about us."

"What makes you think that?" Natalie demanded anxiously. "Has she said anything to you?"

"She hasn't spelled it out. But a woman of her age is past mistress of the arch hint, the little innuendo, the look that speaks a whole dictionary. I think, Natalie, that you might have overextended yourself, wangling this invitation for the weekend. It's given your patroness too many ideas about you and me, and she'll be expecting confirmation in the way we act together."

"That's all in your imagination," Natalie said uneasily. "And as I keep trying to make you understand, Grant, I did *not* wangle the invitation. It came as a total surprise."

He looked at her with that same infuriating amusement. "Can you honestly say that Lady Aston sees our relationship as nothing more than a strictly professional one?"

Natalie lifted her shoulders in an overelaborate shrug. "How am I expected to know what she thinks?"

At that instant Lady Aston called from her card table, "Natalie, dear, why don't you and Mr. Kilmartin take a little stroll to the gazebo? It looks charming now that it's been repainted, like a two-tiered wedding cake, I always think. So romantic in the moonlight."

While Natalie frantically sought for a plausible excuse to refuse, Grant put his hand under her elbow, saying, "Thanks for the suggestion, Lady Aston. We won't be too long."

Celia treated them to an indulgent smile. "Oh, don't hurry, Mr. Kilmartin. It's such a pleasant, warm evening."

Crossing the flagged terrace, Grant retained his grip on her arm until Natalie pointedly drew away.

"Now will you admit that I'm right about Lady Aston?" he demanded with a soft chuckle.

"Listen, I've given her no cause for getting these ideas."

"No? Still, since she *has* got them, there's no sense in our disabusing her . . . yet. We'd better play along."

They had reached the bottom step at the edge of a wide, sweeping lawn, and Natalie stopped abruptly, her hand resting on the stone baluster. "You mean . . . put on a show for Lady Aston's benefit?"

"Makes sense, doesn't it? If it gives her ladyship pleasure to think that she's acting Cupid, it won't help either of us to prove her wrong. Besides, Natalie, we just might find we enjoy it." He gestured to their right. "The gazebo, I think, is in this direction."

"I'm not going to the gazebo or anywhere else with you," she objected.

"Pity. I'll have to go for a stroll on my own. You'd better hang around here and wait for me. You could hardly walk back into the drawing room and blazon to our hostess that we've had a tiff. She'd be bitterly disappointed in you, Natalie."

He had a point there, she acknowledged silently. "Please, Grant, let's just stay here for a few minutes, then go back inside together."

He shook his head. "Lady Aston might ask questions about the gazebo that we couldn't answer."

"Your logic is slipping," Natalie said coldly. "If you're right about the way Lady Aston is thinking, then she would hardly expect us to notice much about our surroundings."

Grant inclined his head. "I stand corrected. Still, I feel like a stroll to work off that sumptuous dinner. So, are you coming with me, or aren't you?"

"Oh . . . very well."

The drift of piano music from the drawing room followed them as they walked in silence across the springy turf, growing ever fainter. The moon cast its gentle light over the gardens, touching the treetops with silver and throwing dense shadows on the ground before them. A sweet scent of honeysuckle and summer jasmine pervaded the evening air, and the soft buzzing song of a nightjar could be heard.

The gazebo was a delicate structure of lacy ironwork, painted white—more like a giant bird cage than a wedding cake, to Natalie's mind. A spiral staircase led to the small upper story, obviously designed as a viewing platform. When they'd climbed up, Natalie could see the landscape for miles, a fairy scene in the moonlight, with pinpoints of light from isolated houses and the occasional flash of a car's headlights on a distant road. An owl hooted eerily from the woods behind them, and she suddenly gave a little shiver.

"What's the matter, are you cold?" Grant's tone was solicitous.

"No, I . . ." She had shivered, she realized, from the fact of Grant's nearness as he came to stand beside her at the rail, the sleeve of his jacket only millimeters from her bare arm. To move away would reveal the shaming truth, so she gritted her teeth and remained where she was. "It's nothing."

He raised his hand and touched her cheek with the back of a finger in an achingly familiar gesture. "You're so tensed up, Natalie."

"I am not tensed up," she flared.

"Why fight it?" he murmured, his face so close to hers that she could feel the warmth of his breath stirring her hair.

"I . . . I don't know what you mean."

He sighed impatiently. "Let's not go back to that stupid game. You had the honesty to admit, that night we had dinner on the river, that you wanted me. So let's start from there. I want *you*, Natalie, you want *me*. The solution is easy."

Her heart was thudding with wild hammerbeats and she knew that her shaky voice betrayed her emotion. "Everything is changed now."

"Not everything, Natalie. Not what matters most."

"How can you say that?" she snapped. "You're mad as hell at me, Grant. You've said some hateful things about my motives, and you've made it horribly clear that you only put up with me as a business associate because you're compelled to, in order to satisfy Sir Matthew's conditions. All right, if we're obliged to work together, let's do it in a reasonably civilized manner. There's no need for us to quarrel—in fact, we should consciously avoid disagreements as something that will jeopardize our professional relationship . . ."

She was babbling, Natalie knew, and she was brought to a stumbling halt by the touch of Grant's hand on her shoulder.

"I believe in facing facts," he observed calmly.

"Isn't that exactly what I'm telling you we should do—face facts?"

He shook his head. "You're suggesting that we should emulate the ostrich . . . a singularly unintelligent bird."

Natalie was gripped by a sense of helplessness. She felt cornered, not by his actual words, but by the resonant timbre of his voice, which was as seductive as a caress. The hand which still rested on her shoulder seemed to burn through the filmy crêpe-de-chine into her bare skin, branding her with his stamp of possession.

"Let's go back to the house," she whispered huskily.

"No, not yet. It's too soon." He laughed softly. "Why should we shatter Lady Aston's romantic illusions about us? Like I said, if we set our minds to it we might even manage to make them a reality."

"Grant, please . . ." she begged. "I tried to explain, that night, how I felt. I . . . I'm still confused. I don't really want an emotional involvement, not with anyone. I just want to be left to get on with my career."

"Which you're doing very effectively," he clipped. "When it comes to maneuvering and manipulating people, Natalie, you could beat most men in top management hands down."

"That's not fair," she cried.

"As a single-minded career woman, you should take it as a compliment."

"But you didn't mean it as a compliment."

In the moonlight his craggy face was an enigma of highlights and dark shadows. "I'd much rather you took *this* as a compliment, Natalie."

His sudden kiss caught her unawares. The hand on her shoulder slid to her waist and she was pulled against his whipcord frame. His lips on hers were soft and warm and coaxing, eliciting an instant, reluctant response from her. As the kiss deepened, his tongue became an erotic probe plunging deep into her mouth. Natalie's thoughts spun in a wild spiral of emotion until she felt dizzy with elation, weak with longing; she knew only that she wanted Grant. All her doubts and reservations had gone rocketing off into the great vortex of the night sky. Her hands crept up to draw him even closer, sliding over the taut, corded muscles of his shoulders. Every cell in her body was exquisitely alive, fire running through her veins and the tangy male scent of his skin filling her nostrils. When they broke away a moment to take breath, she let out a low, shivery moan of delight.

Time had come to a stop for her, and the rest of the world didn't exist. Grant covered her face with kisses, his lips drawing a tingling trail across her velvety skin, lingering at the corner of each eye, tracing the delicate curves of her brows and moving down to the tip of her nose before homing once again on her mouth, devouring her with his passion. And all the while his warm hands roamed across her back, exploring her flesh through the gossamer-thin fabric of her dress so that Natalie felt naked in his arms. Her breasts swelled, their peaks hardening of their own accord until she felt Grant must be just as aware of them pressed against his chest as she was aware of his surging arousal.

"Natalie, you're so lovely," he whispered, drawing back enough to look down into her eyes. "Let me come to your room tonight."

She was silent, an instinctive refusal springing to her lips, but hovering there, unable to shape itself into words. Why should she deny herself the ecstasy his lovemaking would bring? But while she still hesitated, there suddenly came a burst of voices and laughter, as if the rest of the house party were emerging onto the terrace. Natalie stiffened in his arms, and Grant regretfully released her and stood back.

"Their timing could have been better," he muttered savagely.

Natalie's heartbeat was still thudding in her ears. "Let's go," she stammered shakily, "in case they come over this way and find us."

"So what?" he demanded. "We're here, remember, at the specific suggestion of our hostess."

"Yes, but . . ."

"What's the 'but' this time, Natalie?"

In truth, it was because she still felt so shattered, her emotions in such bewildering turmoil, that it seemed impossible to face anyone else and behave normally.

She needed a few minutes alone to try to pull herself together. But she wasn't about to admit that to Grant.

"I must go to my room and check . . . well, my makeup and so forth."

"So that you can give the right ice-maiden image when you present yourself in public again?" he suggested with an ironic laugh. "Not a hair out of place or the slightest lipstick smudge that might hint at the passion boiling behind that prim facade of yours."

Natalie opened her mouth to remonstrate, then thought better of it. She forced herself to speak lightly. "What a big issue you're making out of a casual kiss."

The voices and laughter were drawing nearer and she turned away quickly to descend the spiral staircase and make her escape before it was too late. But Grant caught her arm in a savage grip and jerked her back to face him.

"There was nothing casual about that kiss," he hissed in a low voice that seethed with anger. "It was a promise, Natalie, a pledge. The step that follows is inevitable—you know that as surely as I do. It's as inevitable as summer coming after spring. Now, scoot off to your room or I'll really give these people something to gossip about."

Saturday morning. Reflections of sunlight danced on the surface of the water, and the shimmering heat haze gave a strangely unreal effect to the scene around the pool. Natalie, stretched out on a lounge chair in a white bikini, felt curiously light-headed—the result, she acknowledged ruefully, of a disturbed night rather than the high temperature.

She had drifted through the hours of darkness in a state of restless anger. Remembering Grant's parting words at the gazebo, she had feared that he might try to come to her room. If so, he would find the door locked,

and it would remain locked. How thankful she was now
for the interruption that had saved her from the crazy
impulse to agree to his suggestion. Yet her body denied
the reasoning of her brain that it *had* been a crazy
impulse. Her flesh still tingled where his hands had
caressed her, and she felt an aching void deep within
her.

At breakfast, served as a casual buffet on the sun-
drenched terrace, Grant had helped himself liberally
from the silver chafing dish of kidneys and bacon,
eating with a hearty appetite as though he hadn't a
problem in the world. While Natalie, tense and on
edge, had toyed with just coffee and a triangle of melba
toast. Later, the older houseguests had drifted to the
croquet lawn and the others divided themselves between the pair of immaculately kept grass tennis courts
and the swimming pool.

To protect herself from the need to make conversation with the other people lounging around the pool,
Natalie had let her eyelids droop and was feigning
sleep. Something now prompted her to open them, and
she found Grant framed in her view, poised on the
highest of the three springboards. Relaxed, unhurried,
he took up his stance before diving. Clad in the briefest
navy-blue swim trunks, he looked a magnificent dark-
haired Apollo, having a smooth bronzed skin and the
well-knit musculature of an athlete. His body was
precisely as Natalie's imagination had envisioned it, the
perfection of male virility. Her nerves prickled again
with the memory of Grant's threat, his forecast of
inevitability, made the evening before. So far this
morning they hadn't spoken to each other except in
public.

Grant dived, making a graceful arc and cleaving the
water with scarcely a splash. As she watched him
surface and swim with smooth, easy strokes, she heard

an unexpected noise coming from behind her. Surprised, she glanced around quickly to see two powerful motorcycles approaching across the lawns. They bumped down a grassy slope and came to rest within a few yards of the pool. Four figures in black leather gear dismounted, and it was only when they took off their helmets that she recognized one of the girls as Jodi Aston. Jodi showed no sign of recognizing Natalie, or indeed anyone else. As far as she was concerned, it was as if the group of people already gathered around the pool didn't exist.

"Well, here we are," she said to her companions. "Let's cool off."

Laughing among themselves, they started peeling off their clothes. For a startled moment Natalie thought they were going to strip naked, but it emerged that they were all wearing swim gear underneath.

From the direction of the croquet lawn the agitated figure of Celia Aston came hurrying over. "Hello, Jodi, dear . . . I thought it must be you when I heard all that commotion." She smiled around the group in a vaguely welcoming way. "Well, darling, aren't you going to introduce me to your friends?"

The girl threw her mother a disdainful glance. "We've only come for a swim," she said, and plunged headlong into the pool. The others promptly followed her, and all four started horsing around in the water, not caring that they got in the way of her parents' guests. With a despairing sigh, Celia came and sat down beside Natalie, presumably thinking that she'd better remain at poolside in case things got even more out of hand.

"I'm terribly sorry about this," she murmured with an apologetic smile. "Now you can see for yourself the trouble we have with Jodi."

"Don't worry," Natalie said consolingly. "They're

not doing any harm. It's just four teenagers enjoying themselves."

Grant had climbed out on the far side of the pool. Looking amused, his eyebrows raised inquiringly, he strolled around to where she and Celia were sitting. The sight of his tall, leanly built body streaming with water, the muscles rippling beneath the glossy tanned skin as he moved, brought a husky note to Natalie's voice when she explained to him, "It's just Lady Aston's daughter and some of her friends."

"I do hope, Mr. Kilmartin, that they didn't drive you out of the pool," Celia said anxiously. "They're so noisy and thoughtless . . ."

"Not at all, Lady Aston," he lied politely, with a charming smile. "I was about to get out anyway— tempted by the thought of that bowl of claret cup."

Having checked that no one else wanted any refreshments at the moment, he helped himself from the punch bowl, then stretched his lean frame on the grass beside Natalie. She tried to keep her gaze averted, but found it constantly pulled back to linger on the firm contours of his torso and the long, powerful legs.

After a while the four young people emerged from the water and gathered around the punch bowl, giggling among themselves. One of the boys fished out a cube of ice and pressed it against the bare shoulders of the other girl.

"You rotten pig, Mike," she shrieked, and tried to slap him.

"I thought it might cool you down a bit, Patsy," he snorted.

"Jodi, dear," Celia called uncertainly, "this is Mr. Kilmartin, who is doing the conversion of that warehouse where Daddy and I are going to have the penthouse. And this is Mrs. Kent, whom you met before at the flat, remember?"

The girl ignored Natalie. But Grant, who'd propped himself up on his elbows and nodded hello, she treated to a long, challenging glance from her large hazel eyes. "Hi! There's a question I want to ask you."

"Ask away."

"What d'you reckon you're up to," she threw at him aggressively, "turning a place like that warehouse into fancy-priced apartments?"

He looked back at her with a bland smile. "You know Princess Dock, do you, Jodi?"

"Well . . ." She shrugged. "I've seen it."

"And what would you suggest was done with it?"

"It ought to be left alone," chipped in the boy called Mike, who was dark-haired and quite good-looking when he wasn't scowling, as now.

"You mean, left alone to fall to pieces?" Grant queried equably. "I don't see what good that would do."

"And what good d'you reckon you're doing now?" Mike demanded. "Tarting the place up for the rich."

"Really, Jodi, why are your friends being so rude to my guests?" protested Celia faintly, but Grant held up a placatory hand. "No, Lady Aston, it's a fair enough question and it deserves an answer."

The four youths gathered closer, staring down at him. Quite at ease stretched out on the grass as he was, Grant reached for his glass and took a sip before continuing. "Even the rich have to live somewhere, Mike. And if by providing homes for them we can improve the environment for other people as well, so much the better. Wouldn't you agree?"

"And how are you improving the environment for ordinary folk by doing what you're doing?" growled the second boy, whom the others called Rog.

Grant smiled at him with amusement. "For starters, if I wanted to be personal, I could point out that I'd be showing much more concern for the environment than folks who tear around the country on motorbikes making a rackety noise."

"That's entirely different," Rog snapped.

"Taking a more positive line," Grant went on imperturbably, "I shall be preserving, more or less intact, a fine example of nineteenth-century industrial architecture, which represents the expanding prosperity of the Victorian era. The structure is in a vulnerable condition, and if it were left to deteriorate much further it would have to be demolished for safety reasons . . . to everyone's permanent loss."

"So why not restore it to being a warehouse again? Or," Rog added with a sneer, "make it into flats for *ordinary* people?"

"The answer to your first question is that the day of such large warehouses is past. In order to keep up with modern trends, London's docks have had to change considerably and also move downstream, nearer the sea. So the former dock areas have fallen into disuse. Regarding your second question, Rog, the cost of conversion of such a warehouse building into living accommodation is astronomical . . . an amount that no public-housing authority could even begin to justify. Believe me, the people who're going to live at the new Princess Dock apartments will have to pay heavily for the privilege." He glanced at Celia Aston with a smile. "As Jodi's parents can confirm."

"It's the same old story all over again," Mike protested with a sulky glare. "Money will buy you everything."

"No!" said Celia with sudden, surprising vehemence. "You're quite wrong there, young man. There are many, many things in life that money cannot buy."

"Such as what?" demanded Patsy, who had been silent up until now.

Celia hesitated, then replied with an air of shy defiance, "Such as love, my dear, and health and happiness. I won't suggest that having money isn't a big help in life, but it brings lots of worries and responsibilities at the same time. Whether one is rich or poor doesn't affect the essential requirement for true happiness, which is a sense of being wanted and needed by someone you care about."

Patsy shrugged. "That all sounds very clever, but you still can't justify a scheme like this one, which deprives poor people of housing."

"How will it be doing that?" Grant asked. "I'll tell you this, Patsy, the Princess Dock conversion will provide a lot of much-needed employment in what is at present a decaying area."

"He's got a point there, you know." To Natalie's astonishment, this was from Jodi. The girl was looking at Grant with a sort of awed respect. "When you come to think about it, providing jobs for people is pretty important, isn't it? And what earthly use would it be letting those dockland areas just stagnate?"

Mike laid a hand on her arm. "Leave it alone, Jodi. It's useless to get stuck into this sort of argument. Is there any grub going? I'm starved."

"Oh, all right. We'll go and dig something up from the kitchen." Reluctantly, it seemed, she turned away from Grant and led her friends across the lawns. Lady Aston, saying with a nervous laugh that she'd better see they didn't gobble up everything she'd provided for lunch, hurried after them.

"That kid Jodi's got a crush on you, Grant," called Blanche Skinner, who was lying stretched out on a chair a few feet away. "Is that the effect you always have on young girls? I bet you take maximum advantage of it—eh?"

Grant laughed easily. "I don't go in for babes in arms, Blanche. In any case, I'm sure you're wrong about Jodi. To someone of her age I'm incredibly ancient . . . way over the hill."

Covertly studying his superbly structured frame through lowered lashes, observing how his tanned skin gleamed like polished copper in the sunlight, Natalie found that last statement ludicrous. Grant was a magnificent specimen of proud manhood. There was a sense of potent virility in every muscle of his taut body, in the way he held his head, the set of his broad shoulders that tapered to a slim waist and leanly molded hips, the long length of his powerful legs. The casualness of his relaxed posture at poolside was deceptive. She knew that like a jungle creature in wait for its prey, his body was tuned to perfection; he was capable of springing instantly to his feet, in full command of all his dynamic strength.

Quickly, before her wayward thoughts could lead her into dangerous channels, she rose and went to the pool. She was grateful to manage a neat, clean dive, knowing that Grant was watching her.

That evening brought an influx of local guests, so that the house was crowded. After dinner there was dancing in the grand salon, last night's pianist being joined by bass and drums. Natalie did her best to avoid Grant, as she'd been doing all day, but when he came up while she was chatting to Lady Aston and asked her to dance, she had no option but to accept. Once she was in his arms, held intimately close against him, her sensual longings of the previous evening came sweeping back. Weakly she abandoned herself to the pleasure of dancing with Grant.

Floating in a dreamy daze of happiness, she was surprised when he came to a halt, though the music still continued. Then she saw that he had steered her through the doorway and behind one of the great pillars that supported the domed ceiling of the hall, out of sight of other guests.

"We can't stop here," she said, and tried to pull herself from his encircling arms.

"Why not?" Grant drawled, retaining her slender body against his husky frame with a firm pressure of the hand at her back.

"What . . . what will people think?"

He chuckled softly. "What Lady Aston has been encouraging people to think all this weekend. They'll regard it as only natural that I've brought you out here to kiss you."

"Hard luck, then," Natalie retorted sourly, "because I'm not about to cooperate."

He reproached her with a lazy smile. "That's not very friendly, Natalie. I understood, from what you insisted so vehemently last night, that you didn't rate a casual kiss as all that momentous."

"Last night was last night," she threw back at him wildly, "but this evening I just don't happen to want you to kiss me."

"Liar!" he said with a look that brought a wash of heat to her body. Before she could take evasive action, he had her pinned against the pillar with his weight. When she tried to push him away, he seized her two wrists and held them high above her head, clamping them to the cool marble. His kiss was long and searching, drugging her with pleasure, and gradually her resistance ebbed away. Sensing this, Grant released her hands and she folded her arms around his neck, drawing him closer while their lips clung together in a sweet melding that sent a great warm joy flowing through her. She was dizzily aware of his quickening desire, of his rapid pulse, and her own heart was thudding out a primitive tattoo that seemed to thunder in her ears.

Grant's hands roamed her body restlessly, igniting little fires wherever they touched her . . . skimming across her back and spanning her slim waist caressingly, then sliding down over the curve of her hips to clench into the soft cheeks and jerk her against the thrust of his loins. In a fever of delight her fingers tangled into his dark hair, clawing him to her in a wild abandonment of longing.

The kiss seemed to go on and on deliciously, raising her to new heights of sensual excitement. And when at last Grant drew back a little, he murmured her name again and again in the taut huskiness of his throat. "Natalie . . . sweet Natalie, you can't have any idea what you do to me. I want you so much."

"Oh, Grant," she whispered back, adrift on a stormy sea of passion. She felt no confidence that, had they been somewhere quite alone at this moment, she could have refused him anything.

But they were not alone. This was madness! At any instant someone might appear and be a witness to this outrageously sensual scene. With a determined effort, she pushed against the solid wall of Grant's chest. Reluctantly he gave way and moved back a few inches.

"What's the matter?" he asked in a thick voice.

"We mustn't carry on like this," she said urgently. "Not here, for heaven's sake."

"Where, then?"

"Not anywhere. Please let me go, Grant. We must return to the salon. And don't ask me to dance with you again, because I shall refuse."

"Perhaps you're right," he admitted ruefully. "We ought to go back now. Tomorrow, when we get away from here, we can be alone together."

"Don't start getting any ideas about tomorrow," she warned him, sobering up as her pulse rate became more nearly normal.

"I don't need to, sweetheart. The ideas are already there."

"Then forget them."

He laughed dryly. "You might as well tell me to forget my own name. It can't be done, Natalie."

Later, as she danced with other men—men who probably wondered why she paid so little attention to their complimentary remarks—Natalie felt torn apart, tormented by doubt and uncertainty. She wasn't going to let Grant stampede her into anything. But when the time came that she had to make up her mind about him, did she really have a free choice?

They drove back to London after dinner on Sunday evening. Sir Matthew and Lady Aston seemed entirely sold on the idea of living in the penthouse at Princess Dock, so the weekend could be called a huge success. But it didn't seem that way to Natalie as she and Grant sped through an evening that had turned to rain. Her mind was tuned to the moment, scarcely an hour ahead, when they would swing into the courtyard at Chandler's Wharf. What then? After what had happened between them, it was impossible to believe that Grant would simply say good night and drive away.

Trying to escape the emotional tangle of her thoughts, because she still couldn't decide *what* she wanted, she kept up a flow of conversation about the weekend.

"You dealt very effectively with Jodi Aston yesterday at the pool," she said in a bright voice.

"You think?" Grant slipped down a gear to corner and take the main London road. "She's one muddle-headed kid and needs to be sorted out. Actually, I have a hunch that lurking behind that dropout manner of hers there's an above-average brain."

"You could be right. The Astons are terribly worried about the way Jodi carries on, but I think a lot of the blame lies with them. With Sir Matthew, mainly."

"How come?"

"They had a son a couple of years older than Jodi, did you know? He was very bright, according to Lady Aston, the apple of his father's eye and all lined up to succeed him in the business empire he's built. Then, two years ago, he was tragically killed in a climbing accident."

Grant flickered her a glance. "So Sir Matthew has transferred his hopes and aspirations to Jodi?"

"Right. He wants her to go into Aston Financial Holdings after she finishes at college. But she refuses to listen."

"Instead, she's going out of her way to show that she won't be molded into a substitute for her brother?"

"That's how it looks to me," Natalie said, pleased that he'd followed her thinking. "Jodi's behavior is rude and inconsiderate, but I can't help feeling a sneaking sympathy for her. It's so desperately unfair, trying to change people's characters to fit what you want them to be, instead of accepting them as themselves."

Grant threw her another quick glance. "That came straight from the heart," he commented. "Who was it tried to change *you*, Natalie? Your ex-husband?"

"Yes," she admitted on a whispered breath.

"In what way did he try to change you?"

After a brief hesitation she said reluctantly, "He was older than me, twelve years older, and he expected me to be very poised and assured and capable before all his friends. Maybe I was a bit *too* immature, even for eighteen, but at the time we got married I . . ."

When she didn't continue, Grant said gently, "You had recently lost your parents, hadn't you, so you were vulnerable. In need of sympathetic understanding. If that wasn't forthcoming from your husband, Natalie, then I'd suggest that *he* was the one who lacked maturity."

"Let's not talk about my marriage," she said, wishing now that they'd never got started on this track.

"But it's left scars?"

"I guess. I learned an invaluable lesson, though, and the scars I carry have to be checked against experience."

"What was the invaluable lesson you learned?" asked Grant. "Never to put your trust in a man again?"

So unerringly close to the truth! Nervously she skated away from giving him a direct answer. "I learned to put my trust in myself—in my own ability. Just like every successful man does."

Grant was silent, his fingers lightly turning the wheel as he pulled out to pass another car. Then he said, musingly, "Remember Professor Higgins' heart cry in *My Fair Lady* . . . 'Why Can't a Woman Be More Like a Man?' It's not a philosophy I subscribe to."

"Because you believe in the inherent superiority of men?" she flashed.

"Wrong, Natalie," he said in a serious voice. "I support the idea of equality one hundred percent . . . of equal *rights* for women. But I'm dead against the idea of women trying to ape men in every darn thing they do. Why deliberately reject the feminine qualities such as tenderness and gentleness, sympathetic understanding and a general attitude of caring about other people's feelings—qualities that men so often lack altogether?"

"Pretty words, Grant. It would nicely suit men like you, wouldn't it, to disarm us in the battle for equality? What you really want is to keep us just as sex objects—wives, and mothers of your children."

"Wrong again!" He gave a dry, humorless laugh. "I tried marriage, if you remember, and I found it a sad disappointment. If either one of us was used as a sex object, it was me, not Melissa." There was a note of suppressed rage in his voice, and oddly, despite herself, Natalie felt a kind of sympathy for him steal over her. They had both been through a disastrous marriage, and for the first time she could see this fact as a link between them.

"What went wrong in your case?" she found herself asking.

"It's a long story," he clipped tersely, "and this isn't the right moment."

The courtyard at Chandler's Wharf was rainswept and deserted when they drove in. Grant parked as near as possible to her front door, and cut the engine and headlights. Then, without speaking, he turned slowly in his seat to look at her. His eyes were two shadowed pools, yet they seemed to blaze with the unspoken question.

The moment had arrived and the decision was hers to make. A flurry of panic raced through her and her heart began a wild pounding, the blood surging in her veins. Her mouth suddenly felt dry and she swallowed nervously. Grant waited, the silence stretching interminably, while she fought with the opposing messages her brain and her body were frantically sending out. She looked back at Grant, mesmerized, seeing only the silhouette of his head and shoulders against the pale glow from one of the courtyard lamps. He was, terrifyingly, a menacing force that threatened to destroy her; yet in those same throbbing moments, he offered the promise of blissful fulfillment beyond anything she had ever known.

At long last she heaved a deep, shuddering sigh. Of defeat? Of victory? She didn't know. Her voice came faintly through the tightness of her throat.

"Would . . . would you like to come in for a cup of coffee, Grant?"

Chapter Seven

Grant was sitting on the sofa when she emerged from the kitchen carrying the tray. The room glowed warmly in the light of a single shaded lamp, each piece of furniture casting a soft shadow. He had slipped off his jacket and tie, Natalie noted, so that his shirt was loose at the throat. She shivered slightly at the thought of his molded chest and shoulders beneath the shirt, wanting to pass her fingertips across the smooth tanned skin, knowing how beautiful it would feel to her touch.

"That coffee smells good," he said, smiling at her, watching her face.

"You should feel honored," she quipped as she set the tray on a low table. "I took the trouble to make real for you again, instead of instant."

She sat down beside him on the sofa, careful to keep a clear foot of space between them. Her hand trembled so much as she poured that it was a job to stop the coffee from spilling into the saucers. Grant reached forward and took his cup from her, then leaned back against the cushions. Nervously she began babbling inanities—about the weather, about the thriller she was reading, about a film on Chinese art that had been televised recently. Still Grant smiled, watchfully, enigmatically, as he sipped his coffee. At length he put down his cup, reached out and took hers and put that down also.

"I feel almost afraid to touch you," he said with a

rueful twist to his lips. "I long to hold you, Natalie, to make love to you, but I'm scared you might suddenly vanish into thin air like a beautiful bubble."

"Oh, Grant . . ." she whispered huskily.

The next instant she was locked in his arms. Her heart gave a leap of joy and all her doubts and nervousness went skittering away like autumn leaves before a sudden breeze. It felt so unbelievably right, so unbelievably wonderful. She wound her arms around his neck and drew him closer, while his hands slid sensuously over her warm curves. She was aware, with a dizzying sense of elation, of Grant's quickening desire, and his heartbeat was as rapid as her own.

There was no counting the minutes as they clung together, their senses drugged by the passion of the kiss, yet to Natalie it felt as if every nerve end was tinglingly alive with expectation, with longing. His fingertips, one moment feather-light in their caresses, then hard and demanding as they kneaded her soft flesh, drew patterns of swirling pleasure around her body. Her skin glowed, liquid fire ran along her limbs, and her breasts felt swollen and heavy in the gentle cupping of his hands, the nipples hardening to peaks of exquisite torture under the tender, cruel flicks of his thumbs.

"Tell me," he murmured deep in his throat, "tell me that you want me."

"Yes, Grant, I want you," she whispered.

With a cry that was half-triumph, half-impatience, he lifted her in his arms and carried her through to the bedroom, laying her upon the downy softness of the duvet. With quick, sure hands he unzipped her yellow dress and slid it from her shoulders, then pulled it away over her hips and free of her legs until she lay in just her bra and panties. He paused then, gazing down at her in the golden glow that streamed through the open bedroom door, as if his eyes were drinking in her slender loveliness, savoring this precious moment. Then, with a little smile playing on his lips, he swiftly removed the last two wisps of fabric, exposing her full naked beauty.

"You're exquisite," he breathed. "As perfect as I guessed you'd be, as I knew you must be."

Natalie could sense the trembling of his restrained passion as he ran his two hands erotically from her shoulders, over the mounds of her breasts and across the tender softness of her stomach. A sweet tension was radiating through her, making her bones melt and driving out all shyness. Instead, she felt a sense of wild exultation at the intensity of his desire for her, plainly reflected now in the molten glow of his eyes.

With his gaze still upon her, Grant rose and stripped off his own clothes, dropping them to the floor where he stood. Natalie in turn feasted her eyes upon the superb body she had watched with such wonderment yesterday at Hartwell Manor when Grant was poised, bronzed and magnificent, on the diving board, and afterward, lazily at ease with his smooth, rippling skin just inches from her yearning fingers, when he was lounging on the grass beside her chair. Now even the brief concealment he'd worn then was gone. He towered above her, breathtaking in his virility, for a few more moments of tormenting expectancy. Then, with a quick catch of breath, he stretched his lean length beside her on the bed, his arms sliding around her, his mouth against hers, his lips teasing and demanding, his tongue a tantalizing probe as he tasted her sweetness.

For long, delirious minutes they struggled on the bed . . . struggled not as enemies, but as eager protagonists seeking the intimate contact of every last square inch of their bodies, warm flesh pressed to warm flesh. Natalie gloried in the throbbing urgency of his arousal against her yielding softness.

Unhurriedly, seeming intent only upon her pleasure, Grant continued to reverence her body with his hands, his lips, his tongue, murmuring her name as an added caress, finding new exciting sensations for her in every soft curve, every secret crevice, rousing her toward higher and still higher peaks of delight. When his questing mouth fastened on a tingling nipple, tugging and teasing and rolling it between his lips, she cried out in delirious joy. She felt in a haze of bliss as his wandering hand moved downward and began a slow circling movement ever nearer to the central core of her womanhood.

"Sweet Natalie," he murmured. "How gloriously soft your flesh is . . . soft and smooth, like silken velvet."

She was on the very brink of ecstasy when Grant finally rolled onto her and merged their two bodies, sweeping her up in a wild spiral of escalating rapture to a heavenly explosion of delight. She clung to him breathlessly in a daze of joy and gratitude.

"Dear, sweet Natalie," he murmured again drowsily as they lay together in the contented aftermath of love.

"Oh, Grant!" she whispered into the curve of his neck.

Later, when Natalie opened her eyes from a state of floating half-awareness, it was to see Grant's face beside her on the pillow, the chiseled planes and angles of his features softer in repose. Stealthily she reached up her hand to stroke the smooth warm skin at the base of his throat. To her confusion, his lids sprang open at once, and the dark eyes regarded her tenderly.

"I . . . I'll make some coffee," she said, moving away from him, though she dreaded the naked walk across the room to fetch her robe. But Grant caught hold of her and drew her back to him.

"What a girl you are for making coffee," he said with

a teasing grin, his eyes glinting meaningfully. He pulled her closer against him, and Natalie felt his body quicken with resurging desire.

"Already?" She laughed softly.

His hand ran a flare path of excitement down her spine. "Sweetheart, when you've kept me waiting for so long, you can't expect me to be so quickly satisfied."

As he kissed her gently, and then more firmly, Natalie happily gave herself again to the bliss of his lovemaking, letting him bring her to a high peak of passion that matched and equaled his own. His lean, sensitive fingers played over her back and slid caressingly down the smooth curve of her hips, then clenched the soft flesh of her buttocks, sending ripples of delight pulsing through her. When she felt she could bear the beautiful agony no longer, he took possession of her again and their bodies moved together in joyous harmony, his mouth covering hers, their tongues sweetly tangling. Until once more the stars cascaded in a burst of jeweled glory. It seemed an endless night of loving, of giving and receiving pleasure, and time and again Natalie was carried to the crest of rapture. And afterward they lay together, touching one another tenderly, murmuring each other's names and uttering little wordless sounds of deep contentment. Finally, at some point in the lost hours of that long night, they fell into a deep sleep.

Reflections of morning sunlight flickering on the ceiling greeted Natalie as she slowly opened her eyes. She was drowsily conscious of a warm, golden feeling of happiness. Then, hearing a slight sound, she turned her head to see Grant standing by the foot of the bed, buttoning his shirt. He looked down at her and smiled.

"Hi, sleepyhead!"

All drowsiness gone, she felt a deep sense of embarrassment as memories of the night came flooding back. "What . . . what time is it?" she stammered.

"Late, I'm afraid," he said ruefully, and glanced at his wristwatch. "Eight-forty-one, to be precise. I've barely got time to get home and shaved and changed before a nine-thirty appointment with a client. I'd love to stay and eat a leisurely breakfast with you, but that's out."

Natalie gave a nervous giggle. "After what you said, dare I suggest making you a cup of coffee?"

His answering grin flashed a clear pathway to her heart. "Actually, I'm longing for a cup, but I really must rush." He began tucking his shirt into the waistband of his trousers, then paused, gazing down at her with a glow of desire in his eyes. "I'm tempted to say to hell with everything and get back into that warm bed with you."

"No," she said hastily. "It would be discourteous not to turn up for your appointment."

He stood a moment smiling at her with longing. Coming forward, he sat down on the edge of the bed beside her. Then, holding her two hands captive, he bent to touch his lips first to one rosy peak and then the other. An echo of last night's ectasy rippled through her, and she uttered a shivering sigh of pleasure.

"Grant, you mustn't . . . you have to get going. I thought you were in a hurry."

"Not that much of a hurry," he murmured.

With one fingertip he traced the delicate outline of her mouth, then ran a sensuous trail down over her small pointed chin and the creamy softness of her throat to the valley between her breasts. He would have continued lower, but Natalie jerked away in a convulsive flinch. Illogically perhaps, it seemed to her that Grant was taking unfair advantage of his hypnotic power over her, claiming an indisputable right of access to her body.

"Expect me at seven-thirty this evening," he said. "We'll go out to dinner somewhere first, and then . . ."

"I . . . I'm not sure if I can manage this evening," she faltered.

"*Be* sure!" Grant rose to his feet and started putting on his necktie. "If you've already made other plans, cancel them. You're spending this evening with me—and the night that follows. Understand?" Shrugging into his jacket, he came back to give her a last quick kiss on the forehead. Then he was gone.

The moment the aura of his presence was no longer with her, the tiny niggle of doubt about him swelled until it became a large dark cloud. Hadn't Grant been more than a bit too sure of himself, altogether too complacent? As if, by his ultimate possession of her last night, he had branded her as his personal chattel.

This unhappy thought festered in Natalie's mind during her breakfast of toast and coffee, and remained as the morning wore on. A little before noon, too restless to settle to any of the planning jobs on hand, she decided to go out and spend an hour or so at one of the showrooms looking at the new ranges of upholstery fabrics. At least it would be doing something useful.

As she stepped out of the front door, Diane was standing in the courtyard outside her bow-front display window, critically studying a new arrangement of her glassware. "What d'you think?" she called. "Is it okay?"

"Looks fine to me," said Natalie, strolling over to join her. "I like that bowl with the Grecian figures around it. That's a new style for you, isn't it?"

"Yes, I got the idea from a frieze at the British Museum." She glanced at Natalie and grinned. "Congratulations."

"For what?" Natalie could guess, though, and her cheeks flared with color.

"For coming to your senses at last and letting things

develop with Grant Kilmartin. I saw him leave this
morning." Diane sighed wistfully. "He certainly is one
gorgeous hunk of male. Lucky girl! I hope you can keep
it going for a while."

Natalie threw her friend a freezing look, defying her
to say a single word more on the subject. "I'm in a
hurry," she lied. "I have to meet someone."

She walked off briskly, a sick feeling in her stomach.
Meeting Diane had reminded her afresh of Grant's
track record where women were concerned. That very
first time they'd talked about him, Diane had spoken of
the string of Nordic-type blondes he'd been involved
with since his marriage had broken up, and she'd added
speculatively, "It looks as if he's decided to extend his
range a bit now, with you."

That's all last night really meant to him, Natalie
thought wretchedly—a new experience. Or rather the
same, very familiar experience given a new twist. And
so far as she could judge, Grant had been well pleased
with his experiment—enough, at any rate, to want to
continue the affair with her for a while. It didn't bother
him that there was no affinity between them in other
respects. According to Grant's amoral philosophy, it
wasn't necessary to like or even to trust one's sexual
partner. Desire was his one and only criterion. The
very idea of being seriously involved with someone, of
falling in love, was anathema to him.

Falling in love . . . From where had that thought
sprung? Not, surely, from her stormy relationship with
Grant. She had finally gone to bed with him last night
on *his* terms, for the simple gratification of a sexual
craving. Just that.

And yet, could she have given herself to a man for
whom she cared nothing? Could she possibly have
found such wild, abandoned delight in Grant's arms last
night if she had felt no sense of commitment toward

him? The realization made Natalie slow her steps, and she came to a halt, staring unseeingly into a shop window. The answer was hammering in her brain. What she had believed to be no more than an act of sexual gratification for them both had for her been a demonstration of love. She loved Grant Kilmartin, she ached with love for him. Without love on her part, she knew now with piercing clarity that last night could never have occurred. Her carefully argued logic that a brief affair with Grant would get him out of her system now rang as hollow mockery. Against her will, she had fallen in love with him. The joy and the pain of loving Grant would be with her forever.

Following almost instantly came another thought, which chilled her to the bone. With this shattering revelation about herself, last night must never be allowed to happen again. She and Grant had gone to bed together for the first and the last time. Loving him as she did, she could not accept his casual, uncaring lust. She closed her eyes against this new intensity of misery, fighting back tears.

"Natalie, by all that's wonderful!" The familiar voice right behind her came from days long gone by—the days of her marriage.

"Dudley!" She spun around, staring at him in blank astonishment. "What are you doing here . . . in London?"

"I've come back to settle here. I've had enough of New Zealand." He stood there smiling at her, tall and handsome. The intervening years had added a light brushing of gray at his temples, but his curly brown hair still grew as thickly as ever. "You look marvelous, Natalie," he said with a warm smile, "and it's incredible to bump into you like this. I only arrived home two days ago. I intended to look you up to see how the world's been treating you, then lo and behold, I spot you gazing fascinatedly into a shop window full of technical equipment. Have you become an electronics wizard since we were together?"

"Oh . . . I didn't really notice what sort of shop it was. I was thinking about something else."

Dudley grinned. "It must have been something serious."

Natalie made an effort to get herself together. She felt dazed and weak at the knees with this second shock coming so quickly on top of the sudden realization about her feelings for Grant. "You look well, Dudley," she blurted, which was no more than the truth. His skin had an outdoor glow that she didn't remember from the past.

"Sure, it's a healthy life in New Zealand, but I got a hankering for home. So I decided to come back."

"What about your wife?" she queried, noting that he'd been saying "I" rather than "we." "Isn't she with you?"

Dudley pulled a face. "That didn't work out."

"You've split up?"

"Yes, Jennifer and I are divorced."

"I'm sorry," she murmured conventionally, not knowing what other comment to make.

"There's no cause for regrets," he said, adding with grim humor, "Splitting up with Jennifer was the most sensible thing I've done in my life. She was totally unlike you to look at, Natalie, and perhaps that explains why I married her . . . on the rebound, so to speak. It didn't take me long to discover that she was unlike you in just about every other particular, too. She was a thoroughly hard and selfish woman—all take and no give." He broke off, and added, "Look, we can't talk here in the street. Let's go and sit down over a cup of coffee somewhere."

Natalie hesitated. But, heavens above, she thought, anger and bitterness couldn't be allowed to last forever.

Surprisingly, now that she was actually face to face with her ex-husband, the bitterness she had nurtured these past years was no more than a faint echo. It all seemed so long ago now, hardly real. Yet Dudley had played a vital role in her life. They'd shared a lot together, even if their marriage had ended in disaster. Somehow she couldn't just turn and walk away from him, leaving so many questions unanswered.

"A cup of coffee would be nice," she said with a smile.

They walked together along the street till they came to a suitable place. It wasn't until they were halfway through the door that Natalie realized it was the Café Napoli. But it hardly mattered. She smiled in response to a greeting from the white-aproned Signore Gaspari behind the long counter; then, as she and Dudley sat down, she spotted Riccardo sitting at another table near the service door at the rear. He was here for his lunch, as usual, taking the chance to chat with Maria each time she passed in and out from the kitchen. Natalie gave Riccardo a friendly wave, but she didn't attempt to introduce the two men.

"You seem to be well known in here," Dudley commented in surprise. "Do you come here often?"

"Not really. But that chap at the table over there is my next-door neighbor. He's engaged to the owner's daughter."

"Sensible man!" With a grin, Dudley glanced around the café. "This looks a prosperous place, and he's got his foot nicely in the door."

"It's not like that," she said heatedly. "In fact, he and Maria have had a very hard time. Riccardo makes cameos, and he does the most beautiful carvings. He was doing very well in Italy and they were about to be married. But then Maria had to come to England because her mother was taken ill, so Riccardo followed her here, and—"

Dudley put up his hand to check her. "Save it, you've made your point. I'm not really interested in the life history of your next-door neighbor. I'd much rather talk about you, Natalie." He chuckled. "It takes me back—you always used to spring to people's defense like that if you thought I'd misjudged them."

"Which you often did," she couldn't stop herself from pointing out.

Maria was busy serving, and the other waitress came up to take their order. Dudley asked for two coffees, then leaned back in his chair and surveyed her approvingly.

"You're looking wonderful, Natalie, quite stunning. I can hardly believe it. You always were beautiful— that's what caught my eye in the first place—but now there's something extra-special. It's more than just beauty and charm. You seem to glow with ripe womanhood, and you have a poise and maturity that were altogether missing before. I want to know all about you. I suppose you're married again?"

"No, Dudley, I haven't remarried."

"I can't believe it. Why not?"

"You could say that one unfortunate experience was enough," she retorted with a spark of resentment.

"*Touché,*" he said lightly. "But that doesn't usually put a woman off for long. There must have been attachments in your life—looking the way you do now, the men must stand in line."

Natalie gave a negative shake of her head. "I've been far too busy to get involved like that."

His look was sharply questioning. "Busy doing what?"

"Building a career." While the waitress returned with their coffee, Natalie reflected that it wouldn't do Dudley any harm to know that the young girl he'd married and found wanting had changed into an assured woman who was capable of running her own successful business. "I'm an interior-design consultant," she added with an unconscious lift of her chin.

He raised skeptical eyebrows. "It sounds very grand, but what does it amount to? The point is, do you make any money at it?"

"I make a decent living." Dudley didn't seem impressed, and she wanted him to be. "The way things are heading, I shall soon be doing very well indeed."

"Is that so?" She had really caught his interest now. "I'd like to hear all about it, Natalie."

"Well, just recently I've been named official design consultant for a big development of luxury apartments converted from a dockland warehouse. It's being backed by Sir Matthew Aston, who's very well known in financial circles. You may have heard of him."

Dudley whistled. "I'll say! He's got his finger in several New Zealand pies. How did you manage to worm your way into his good graces?"

"His wife has been a client of mine for some time," she told him.

"Aha! I always knew you had a clever head on your shoulders."

"Really?" she retorted coolly. "You had an odd way of demonstrating your high opinion of my intelligence, Dudley. The whole time we were married, you never stopped carping at me and criticizing everything I did."

He cast her a pained look. "That was a long time ago, Natalie. Besides, can you put a hand on your heart and deny that my criticism didn't help you to become what you are today? There's no doubt about it, my sweet, in those days you were very immature and inclined to be gauche. Now you're a totally different person. You act like a woman who has the world at her feet . . . and knows it."

Natalie gazed down at her scarcely touched coffee. There was an element of wry truth in what Dudley had said. Could she confidently assert that her bitter experi-

ence of marriage hadn't had any plus effects? But for
spending that painful time as Dudley Kent's wife,
would she ever have had the compulsion to forge
herself into the determined career woman she had since
become?

"Even if you're entitled to any of the credit for what I
am now," she said with a cutting edge to her voice, "I
hardly feel inclined to give you any thanks for it. I went
through a very bad time after our divorce. Still, it was a
long while ago now and there's nothing to be achieved
by reopening old wounds."

"You're right," he agreed quickly. "It's all water
under the bridge. So let's be friends, eh?"

"It would be futile, Dudley. Our relationship is a
thing of the past. Dead and done with."

He wouldn't accept that. "When two people have
been married to each other, their relationship is never
really dead. Don't forget the good times we shared,
Natalie. Okay, so perhaps our divorce was inevitable,
given the circumstances. We both of us made mistakes, and somehow everything went sour. But don't
talk to me about there being nothing left between us.
I've thought about you so often since we parted,
remembering those good times . . . how sweet you
were on our honeymoon, how lovely you felt in my
arms, how much you seemed to need me. Our marriage
wasn't a *total* disaster, was it, not if I can have
memories like that? What about you . . . do you ever
think of me?"

"Why, of course I do, occasionally. But—"

"There you are, then," he said on a triumphant note.

Natalie glanced away to evade the intimate look in
his eyes that was trying to entrap her in old, latent
emotions. At any time, in any circumstances, she would
have found an encounter with Dudley disturbing, but
today, when her mind was spinning with thoughts of
Grant, it was more than she could cope with.

"It's time I was going," she said, reaching for her black patent shoulder bag.

"Must you?" There was heavy disappointment in his voice. "We've hardly had a chance to talk. Can't you stay a little longer—maybe have lunch?"

"I have things to do," she said firmly. "Things that must be done today."

He smiled. "Okay, I won't try to detain you. But let's meet again very soon, Natalie . . . one evening for dinner, when you won't be so rushed."

"No, Dudley." She rose to her feet. "There's no point."

He rose too, and stood surveying her appreciatively. "There's every point from where I'm standing. Listen . . . you're in the phone book, I suppose?"

"Of course, but—"

"Then I'll call you sometime, and we can fix a date."

"Dudley, please . . ."

He signaled for the check. "Which way are you heading?"

"Toward Tottenham Court Road."

"Then I'll stroll with you."

Natalie didn't want that, but she wasn't going to argue with him here in the café, with people looking on.

"If you like," she said with a shrug.

A few yards along, a group of young factory hands, free for their lunch hour, were larking about kicking a ball, heedless of any obstruction they were causing. Dudley slipped a protective hand under her elbow and steered her past. He had always been very attentive and solicitous, she recalled, when they were out walking together. He was right, of course, there *had* been some good times in their marriage, especially in the early days. She had no wish to see him again, after this once, but perhaps their accidental meeting did have its credit side. Her memory, feeding upon resentment and bitterness, had turned him into something of a monster. But now, coming face to face with the reality, she was able to view Dudley in a less harsh light. She could see what had attracted her to him in the first place. He was a good-looking man still, and she'd noticed more than one woman casting an appreciative glance in his direction. He could also be a charming companion when he wanted.

They parted at the corner of Euston Road. "I'll call you, Natalie, very soon," Dudley promised.

"I'd rather you didn't," she protested. "Honestly."

He smiled at her in gentle reproach. Then, unexpectedly, he held her shoulders and kissed her lightly. *"Au revoir,* my sweet, until we meet again."

Chapter Eight

$\mathcal{T}$wice during the afternoon Natalie tried to call Grant to stop him coming that evening. The first time, he was engaged on a transatlantic call and she said she'd phone again in a few minutes. The second time, more than half an hour later because Riccardo dropped in, she learned to her dismay that Grant had gone out and couldn't be reached for the rest of the day.

Riccardo's arrival, heralded by his usual rat-tat-tat at her door, was around three o'clock. But unusually, he didn't walk right in. When Natalie opened up to him, he cautiously stuck his head inside and made expressive eyes. "Is all clear, *cara?*"

"How d'you mean, is all clear?"

He gave her an amiable grin. "From what Maria said, I thought that perhaps your companion at the café would still be with you."

"Well, he isn't," Natalie responded testily. "What did Maria say to give you that idea?"

Riccardo dropped onto the sofa and lay back comfortably, his hands linked behind his head. "Maria took one look at the man—to whom, *cara,* you so clearly did not intend to introduce us—and she said, 'He has an extreme interest in Natalie. Who is he?' And of course I was unable to enlighten her. But we are both very happy for you, *cara."*

"You've got the wrong end of the stick, Riccardo. That man you saw me with is my ex-husband. He's just returned to this country from New Zealand, and we happened to bump into one another in the street this morning."

"Really?" Riccardo's curiosity deepened. "And his wish is that you two should get together again?"

"Rubbish. Just because Dudley and I can meet after all these years and talk like civilized people doesn't mean anything. There's no question of us getting together again."

"Okay, okay, I only inquired. But Maria's judgment on such matters I trust, and she hadn't any doubt that he is very interested in you, Natalie. So the question I am asking myself is, where does the other man fit into the picture?"

"What other man?" she parried wildly.

Riccardo's glance reproached her. "Do you have so many on a string? The man I'm talking about, *cara,* is the one you brought home that day when I was here watching your TV." He chuckled. "You will recall, I imagine, that you tried to deceive him into thinking that you and I had a little romance. His name was Grant something-or-other, was it not? He, too, was extremely interested in you, that was very evident, and I have seen his car here once or twice since. From my observance of him, Natalie, he is not a man to be trifled with. So I think you had better watch your step."

"As far as Grant Kilmartin is concerned," she stated flatly, "I happen to be commissioned by his firm to do some design work for them, and that's all." She prayed that Riccardo wasn't going to call her bluff by announcing that he knew Grant had spent last night with her. But mercifully, it seemed he wasn't aware of this embarrassing fact.

"Maria's wager is on the ex-husband," he said, regarding her judicially. "But then, of course, Maria has not observed the competition. I think I would rather put my money on Mr. Grant Kilmartin."

"You'd lose it, then," Natalie retorted crossly. "And so would Maria, come to that. If you've nothing better to talk about, Riccardo, then scoot. I'm busy."

By evening Natalie was in a real state of jitters. When she opened the door to Grant, she was flustered, trembling, aching with love and longing, but she clung to her resolve as to a lifeline. Grant went instantly to take her in his arms, but she held up a forbidding hand.

"No, Grant!"

A puzzled frown ridged his brow. "What do you mean . . . no?"

"No means no," she said coolly. "You were about to kiss me, and I don't want you to."

After a stunned moment, he muttered, "I don't believe this. What's it all about?"

"I tried to phone you this afternoon," she stammered. "I tried twice. Only the first time you were engaged, and the second time you'd gone out and couldn't be reached."

His dark eyes bored into her. "And if you *had* been able to reach me?"

"I . . . I would have told you not to come this evening."

"I see!" His sculptured mouth tightened into a thin, hard line. "It wouldn't have made the slightest difference if you'd spoken to me on the phone. Whatever you said, I'd still have been here now. I told you, remember, to cancel any other plans you had for this evening."

Natalie glared at him furiously. "You had no right to take it for granted that . . . that I'd be *available* again."

"Hadn't I?" he clipped in a tone of dangerous calm. "I'd have thought I had every right, after last night. You made me all kinds of promises."

"I did no such thing," she protested.

"Not verbally," he agreed, "but in actions. And they

speak louder than words, Natalie. You made me a thousand sweet promises with your lovely body, and left me on a high of expectation. What else do you imagine I've been thinking about all day long except this moment when I could hold you in my arms again? And the night ahead of us? It will be even more wonderful than last night."

"Last night," she said faintly, "was a mistake."

"No," he insisted, shaking his head in emphatic denial. "Last night, for the first time since I've known you, you acted sensibly. Truthfully. That was the real you in bed with me, Natalie, a woman with a warm-blooded, passionate nature."

"You're wrong," she cried frantically. "I . . . I just let myself get carried away, and . . ."

"Then let yourself get carried away again . . . tonight and a hundred more nights."

"No! I . . . I was right in what I said to you before, Grant. You and I are tied professionally—like it or not—but that's where our relationship ceases."

He caught his breath in exasperation. "Need we have a replay of this scene? The fact that we happen to be linked professionally doesn't have anything to do with our personal relationship."

"But it must have!"

"Listen to me," he said severely, his dark eyes looking at her with burning intensity. "Even if that argument had any sort of logic up till now, it doesn't hold water anymore. Our professional association is something I never wanted—it was forced on me by your underhanded maneuverings, which made me as mad as hell. But I've simmered down now. If you were a man, I guess I'd have looked at it differently from the start. I'd have been just as mad, but I'd have accepted it as the way things go in business. I'd maybe even have had a grudging respect for the chap who was able to pull a fast one on me. You've made it clear, Natalie, that you're dead set on proving that you're as capable in your job as any man. So okay. I'll treat you like a man—as far as work goes. Which leaves us free to cultivate the personal side of our relationship quite apart from our working lives. In every other regard, believe me, I can never forget for an instant that you're a woman. A very beautiful woman, for whom I feel an intense desire—just as I know that you desire me. You can't possibly deny it, after what we shared last night. So why shouldn't we enjoy the bliss that we can offer one another?"

Meeting the challenge of his dark gaze, Natalie felt dizzy and faint from the fatal tug of attraction she always experienced in Grant's presence. How was she to answer him? To tell the truth was impossible—that last night she had succumbed to his lovemaking in the mistaken belief she was merely giving way to a physical hunger that needed to be assuaged. But she knew differently now. She knew now what previously, until their night together, she had refused even to consider— that she had fallen in love with him. She knew now that *without* loving Grant she would never have surrendered to him. But the realization of her love had brought with it the certainty that she could never again share such ecstatic intimacy with him. She couldn't bear to give herself in love to a man who had no feelings for her in return, a man who took a coldly practical attitude to the whole subject of sex, who saw it as an amusing pastime or as an essential release of bodily needs without any kind of emotional commitment. No, she thought with a shudder, it was utterly unthinkable that she could explain the truth to Grant and admit that she loved him.

Endeavoring to sound crisp and sophisticated, she said, "Aren't you making a big production of something that's not all that important? Don't let's have a postmortem on last night, for goodness' sake. We both know that a man and a woman choose to go to bed together sometimes without its having any great significance. Even . . . even if they both enjoy the experience, it doesn't mean that they have to go *on* sleeping together. And the plain fact is, Grant, that I don't want to."

He threw her a dark look from beneath his heavy brows. "I'd accept that, if I believed you. I've never tried to force myself on a woman."

"Then kindly don't with me."

"Force doesn't come into it, Natalie. You'll never convince me that you don't want me as much as I want you. When we're together, when I hold you, I can feel your body quivering with desire. Right now, at this very moment, there's a million-volt electric charge between us."

"Don't . . . don't be absurd," Natalie said faintly.

The sight of him standing there so close, so devastatingly virile, sent pulsing waves of heat through her, making her senses swirl. As so often since she'd known Grant, she was fighting herself, fighting her own surging emotions. Memories of last night undermined her ability to argue with him . . . memories of his ardent kisses, with his warm, throbbing body crushing her into the bed, coaxing her to unbelievable delights and sweeping her to a triumphant culmination, when she'd cried aloud with joy and the world had dissolved into a cascade of glittering stars.

She must have cried out now, or made some small whimper in her throat. Grant said, his voice thick with irony, "Absurd, you think? And what if I were to stroke your cheek at this moment? What if I were to take you in my arms again . . ." He moved a step toward her, and she backed away in trembling panic.

"No! No, you mustn't."

"Why not?" he demanded impatiently. "Let me hold you in my arms and then say no to me . . . if you can!

I'll make you a promise, Natalie. If, with my arms wrapped around you, you still insist that you want me to leave, I'll go at once and that will be that. *Finis!* I won't ever bother you again."

Natalie had backed away until she was pressed against her desk. Mutely she gazed up at him, the words she might have uttered frozen in her throat.

"Isn't that a fair enough offer?" Grant persisted sardonically. "All I'm asking for is a practical demonstration of your claim that you don't want any more to do with me."

"It ought to be enough," she muttered hoarsely, "that I'm standing here facing you and telling you to leave."

Grant shook his head. "Not nearly enough. Last night was no one-time thing, Natalie, whatever you try to make out. We both know that. I can't begin to understand your motive in suddenly going cold on me again. Maybe you're playing some devious game," he suggested with a cynical twist to his mouth. "Maybe, throughout our whole relationship, you've been jockeying to secure the maximum career advantage."

"No," she suggested weakly, "that's a vile thing to say."

"Is it, Natalie? Last night either has to be a monumental fake on your part, or it was a genuine expression of how you feel toward me. You can't have it both ways."

"Things change," she faltered. "Feelings change."

"In the space of less than twelve hours?" he persisted remorselessly.

Natalie gathered the last fragments of her courage and faced him boldly, straightening up to her full height. "Yes, feelings can change," she declared. "They can change very suddenly, even in a single day."

His brows drew together in a frown. "It would need to be something cataclysmic, that's for sure, to cause such a reversal of feelings. What's happened, Natalie, to bring about your sudden change of heart?"

What had happened was indeed cataclysmic—a blinding flash of insight that told her she was in love with him. She closed her eyes in pain and pressed her hands to her face. "Just accept what I say, Grant, and go away. Please! I . . . I don't want you here."

There was no immediate reply. In the pulsating silence she heard the thudding of her heartbeat. Then Grant's voice came in a low, tense tone. "If I do go now, Natalie, I won't be coming back."

"That's exactly what I want," she averred, hoping to give conviction to the lie.

This time Grant was silent for so long that she grew a little scared. Dropping her hands and letting her eyelids flutter open, she saw that he was looking at her with an expression of dark perplexity. When he next spoke, his voice was softer, gentler. "Natalie, must we always get into a fight when we meet? If it's something I said to you, if I took you too much for granted, then I'm sorry. But it would be crazy to break things up between us just because of piqued feelings."

"No, it's not that." She tried to think, tried to bring order to the chaos of her mind. What could she say to him that he would believe? "Listen . . . I don't deny that I find you attractive, Grant. But that isn't enough in itself."

"Attractive! There's a hell of a lot more than attraction between you and me."

Natalie caught her breath, hoping against all hope that it meant he cared for her, even that he was beginning to love her a little. But when Grant continued, she felt a bitter disappointment. "I've felt attracted to any number of women, and no doubt you have to a lot of men. But not to the same incredible degree. Last night was sensational—the most fantastic love-making I've ever experienced."

She pounced on the word in her bitterness. "'Love-making,' you call it?"

"Would you prefer me to use a cruder word?" Grant retorted in a voice that cracked like a whip. He was repentant at once. "I'm sorry, Natalie, but you provoke me into hitting back. Let's forgive and forget the rotten things we've said to each other, and just remember how good it is when we're together."

He stepped closer, his eyes trapping hers in their sensuous grasp, his arms held out to her invitingly. Natalie gave a shudder of alarm. How could she resist Grant now if he actually touched her, if he kissed her? Already she felt dizzily enveloped in the aura of vibrant warmth that seemed to radiate from his virile body like the heat of a blazing fire; her flesh was tingling as though he were actually caressing her with his lean, strong fingers.

"Damn you, Grant," she said chokily.

"Damn me for what?" he asked in a grating voice. "For existing? For living and breathing and tempting you to act like the passionate woman you are?"

She shook her head weakly, feeling faint with the strength of her longing. The floor seemed to tilt beneath her feet, and she swayed. Grant caught her by the shoulders and held her steady, pressed against the sturdy wall of his body.

"Welcome back, darling," he murmured, wrapping his arms around her tenderly and hugging her close as he buried his face in the fragrant silk of her hair. "This feels so wonderful, so right."

Natalie leaned against him joyously, throwing all resistance to the winds, incredulous now that she'd ever *tried* to resist him. Her arms slid around his neck and she clung to him fiercely, raising her face to receive his kiss.

While their mouths remained locked together, his hands moved over her body, sensuously exploring it through her thin cotton dress, molding the slender bones and soft flesh. Each kneading caress found a sensitive spot that brought Natalie a fresh explosion of delicious sensation.

"Oh, Grant, Grant . . ." she moaned.

His lips began tracing out a weaving pattern of erotic, arousing kisses, his tongue tasting the sweetness of her skin at the dimple of her chin, the curving line of her jaw, the inner shell of her ear. Pushing her hands under his jacket, Natalie pressed her palms to the warm, pulsing flesh of his chest, and felt his thudding heartbeat. She slipped her arms around his waist and let her hands spread out across the breadth of his back, delighting in the feel of iron-strong muscles beneath his shirt. Her fingertips found the channel of his spine and followed it down, so that Grant groaned aloud with desire. Natalie felt the urgent tautening of his need for her, and she was filled with a sense of wonder and happiness that she could bring him so much pleasure.

She was pliant, unresisting, when Grant sat her down on the sofa and pressed her back into the billowy cushions, his hands impatiently seeking the fastenings of her dress. She was lost in a raging fire of excitement and wanting that had destroyed all rational thought. . . .

At that instant, someone rapped on the front door.

"Who the devil would that be?" Grant demanded with a scowl.

"I . . . I don't know," she faltered. "One of the neighbors, I imagine."

His glance burned into her. "Get rid of them, Natalie, whoever it is."

Straightening her clothes and smoothing her hair, she tried to pull herself together, tried to calm her trembling. On legs that felt boneless, she crossed the room and opened the door. To her astonishment, Dudley was standing there, smiling at her. In his arms he held a huge bouquet of red roses.

"Oh . . . hello!" she stammered.

Dudley stepped over the threshold, holding out the flowers to her. In her bewildered state she took them, cradling them in her arms. Then, before she realized his intention, he bent and planted a light kiss on her cheek.

"I've got a taxi waiting, my sweet, and I've reserved a table for two at the Danse Macabre. How . . . ?" He broke off abruptly, suddenly noticing Grant. "Oh, I didn't realize you had someone here."

Natalie, dismayed at the first sight of Dudley, now saw his arrival as a godsend, a chance to escape from a precarious situation with Grant that she'd never intended to let happen. "This is Mr. Kilmartin," she explained with pseudo-brightness. "He's the man I was telling you about, who's developing the dockland warehouse into a block of luxury apartments."

"Oh, I see." Dudley looked relieved, obviously deceived by her performance. "That's quite a project you've got there, Mr. Kilmartin, by all accounts."

Grant's eyes were molten with anger. "No doubt Natalie has also filled you in about what a nice fat killing she herself is going to make from it. She's an extremely clever woman, as perhaps you'll already have discovered." He looked again at Natalie, his furious gaze lingering, drilling deep into her soul. "I don't think we have anything more to discuss, so I'll leave you to enjoy a pleasant evening. Good night!" Without another glance at Dudley, he strode briskly to the door. It slammed behind him, and a few moments later she heard his car roar into life.

Dudley looked at her inquiringly. "He seemed a bit short on temper, darling. Did I interrupt a row or something?"

"It was nothing important," she lied frantically.

"We . . . we just happen to look at things in a different way, and . . . and it inevitably means that we keep having arguments."

Luckily, Dudley accepted that at face value and didn't press for details. "I expect you'd like to dress up a bit before we go out," he said with a grin. "How about putting on something fabulous that'll make every other man in the restaurant envy me like mad?"

Natalie shook her head. "No, I don't think I want to go out with you, Dudley."

"Oh, come on, my sweet," he said coaxingly. "I can promise you a slap-up dinner, and we can yarn about the good times we shared . . . like two old friends."

Natalie stared at him blankly, not really taking in what he was saying. Her thoughts were with Grant, who had departed in such a black fury. She wished now that she'd not seized upon the opportunity to give him a wrong impression. Why hadn't she at once introduced Dudley as her ex-husband, who was merely paying her a visit now that he was back in England? Goodness knows what Grant would have made of the situation. From the bouquet of red roses and Dudley's general demeanor, he would probably assume that they were having an affair. So he would now be imagining that she was the sort of woman who liked to run two men at a time.

One thing: she had succeeded in getting rid of Grant—that was a relief. But she dreaded their next encounter, which would inevitably occur quite soon in the course of her work on Princess Dock. She could envision only too well the look of scathing contempt in those dark eyes of his, the clipped indifference with which he'd speak to her in the future.

"So how about it, darling?" Dudley prompted, looking at her in a puzzled way. "Shall I tell the taxi to wait while you get ready?"

"Oh . . ." Natalie shook herself, trying to focus her attention. She was framing a refusal in her mind when she had second thoughts. Why *not* have dinner with Dudley? Better than to stay at home alone, brooding over Grant and what might have been between them if only . . . if only his attitude toward women had been less cavalier, if only she hadn't been so foolish as to fall in love with him. After all, she argued, wasn't it only civilized to be on reasonably good terms with one's ex-husband? It was a long time now since their acrimonious divorce, and the worst of her painful wounds had healed over.

"Okay, Dudley," she agreed with a quick smile. "I'd like to have dinner with you. Er . . . pour yourself a drink while you're waiting. I won't keep you long."

"Great!" He chuckled. "I'd never have dreamed, twenty-four hours ago, that I'd be taking you out to dinner tonight, Natalie, darling."

The Danse Macabre was the "in" place at the moment. It was packed, and she wondered how Dudley had managed to reserve a table at such short notice. But that was typical of him. He always seemed to know how to pull strings to get what he wanted.

They had cocktails in the lounge, a dim cavern with a fake vaulted ceiling. Huge blown-up photographs of ballet stars—Pavlova, Karsavina and Nijinsky, Fonteyn and Nureyev—were dramatically spotlit amid a wild profusion of trailing greenery. Somewhere in the shadows a pianist played softly.

"That guy Kilmartin . . ." Dudley mused. "He sure was in a rage about something. He hasn't got any fancy ideas about you, Natalie, has he?"

"Of course not," she insisted, hoping that the hot color she felt rushing to her cheeks wasn't giving her away.

"It wouldn't be so surprising, you know," he said, looking at her with warm appreciation. "You're a very lovely woman, my sweet. A very desirable woman."

Natalie sighed. "Let's get this straight at the outset, Dudley. It's nice to have dinner with you, but please don't flirt with me. I'm not in the mood for that. I'd like it if we can just be friends."

"That's all I expect, darling," he assured her quickly, "so don't get me wrong. But what attracted me to you in the first place applies with double force now. I'd be a liar if I didn't tell you that you look sensational, and I'm proud to be your escort. It makes me realize that I was a crass idiot to let you slip through my fingers. Still, it's no use crying over spilled milk."

"I'm glad you see it that way," Natalie said in a subdued voice.

"Mind you," he continued reflectively, "when we get to know one another better again . . . who knows?"

"I don't envisage that we'll be seeing a lot of each other, Dudley." She made her tone brisk, anxious to discourage him from building any kind of hopes around her. "I'm far too busy."

"Now, that I refuse to believe." He laughed. "You're much too intelligent to spend your entire time hard at work, without allowing yourself a chance to relax and enjoy yourself sometimes."

Ice clinked in the tall glass as Natalie picked up the vodka and tonic he'd ordered for her. "There'll be more time for me to relax when I'm better established in my career and I can feel secure."

"I don't think you need worry on that score," Dudley said smoothly. "I made one or two inquiries about you today, my sweet. The word is that you're a bright girl who's really going places."

Natalie couldn't help feeling pleased. "Who was it you spoke to?" she asked.

He smiled mysteriously. "People."

"I don't see why you bothered."

"No? I wanted my own judgment confirmed, that's why I bothered. I've always had a very high opinion of your ability and intelligence, Natalie. As well," he added softly, "as of your beauty."

The waiter came at that point to tell them that their table was ready. Walking through to the restaurant—an extravaganza of decor in vivid jewel colors like a stage set for a ballet—she was conscious of eyes following them. She looked pretty good, she knew, in her floaty chiffon dress of softest coral, worn with strappy gold sandals, and without doubt Dudley was one of the most handsome men in the room.

The food matched the style of the place; it was superb in every detail. They both began with Russian caviar because, he reminded her, she had first tasted it the night he proposed. To follow they ordered *boeuf en croute* with artichoke hearts. And to drink, he was emphatic, nothing but vintage French champagne would match the occasion. With a pang, Natalie's mind fled back to the evening on the riverboat with Grant. Then too it had been champagne for a special occasion. To keep her mind from dwelling on that, she asked Dudley about himself. What did he intend doing now that he was back in England?

"I'm setting up in the import-export business again," he told her. "I've already put out feelers, and there's plenty of scope for someone with drive and initiative. I can do a lot better here than I did in New Zealand." He gave her an intent, meaningful look. "A lot better in every direction. I was a fool, way back, and I didn't realize how good things were for me then."

"Please, Dudley," she protested, uneasy at the direction the conversation was taking. When he suggested dancing, she nodded, and they moved onto the small rectangle of polished parquet. The tempo changed abruptly and the slow number that followed gave Dudley an excuse to hold her close. She tried to draw back a little, but his grip was too strong. "Cheek to cheek," he murmured. "Like the old days, darling. Remember, on our honeymoon? It was good then, wasn't it?"

A heady time, that, when she had believed herself happily in love. And only found out her mistake later. Now she was in love again, with another man, but this time she knew in advance that there could be no happiness for her—not with Grant Kilmartin.

"I never stopped loving you, Natalie, darling," Dudley murmured into the softness of her hair.

"Please," she whispered, "don't talk like that."

"But it's true," he insisted.

"No, Dudley, it isn't true." Annoyed, she was about to tell him to take her back to their table, when from the blur of faces circling around them one face suddenly sprang into sharp focus. It was Grant, and he was dancing with a stunning blonde. Across the floor, through the swaying heads of other couples, their eyes met and locked. The bitter brilliance of his glance made Natalie catch her breath. This was no chance encounter, she knew. Grant had come here deliberately, having overheard Dudley give the name of the restaurant. From somewhere he had summoned this woman —one of the numerous girlfriends he could call on, no doubt—to join him at short notice in order to demonstrate to Natalie Kent how little he cared about her rejection of him earlier this evening.

Unknowingly, she had gone stiff in Dudley's arms, and he remonstrated, "Hey, darling, loosen up and give a little."

For a few moments longer Natalie danced like a mechanical doll, staring blindly into space, anywhere but in Grant's direction. Then suddenly she made up her mind and became supple and clinging in Dudley's arms, laying her face against his shoulder. Pleased, he touched his lips to the silken cloud of her hair again and whispered softly, "That's right, my sweet. Now we can really enjoy ourselves."

Back at their table, Natalie radiated animation, talking brightly and laughing at Dudley's slightest attempt at humor. She longed desperately to ask him to bring the evening to an end and take her home, so that she could nurse her misery alone and fight back against the tumult of jealousy which at this moment was deluging her senses and making her feel faint. But she refused to allow Grant such an easy victory. She would outstay him, to prove how untouched she was by his presence. She danced again and again with Dudley—he had always been a good dancer—and each time she threw herself enthusiastically into the mood of the number, letting her body move smoothly and pliantly to his lead. Fortunately, Dudley seemed to be enjoying himself too much to notice that all her attention was focused on another man in the restaurant.

At long last Grant and the blonde rose from their table and walked across to the exit. Natalie noticed that he didn't so much as glance in her direction. Emotionally drained by now, she at once suggested to Dudley that it was time to go.

"Sure," he agreed amiably, and signaled for the check, paying the large amount without a second look. The doorman found them a taxi, and soon they were whirling across London toward Chandler's Wharf. "I shall have fixed myself up with a car in a couple of days," he told her as he settled back comfortably and, as if casually, slipped his arm around Natalie's shoulders. She noted his frown as she pulled away, but he made no comment.

"You haven't mentioned where you're staying at the moment, Dudley," she said chattily, attempting to keep the conversation in low key.

"It's a small hotel near Grosvenor Square. Not a bad little place. It'll do me until I find what I want."

"Are you looking for an apartment?"

"That's right." He reflected a moment. "What about Chandler's Wharf?"

"There's nothing vacant there," she said hastily. That wasn't true. Riccardo would be leaving in three weeks' time and was actively looking for someone to take over the rest of his lease. But having Dudley as her next-door neighbor was unthinkable.

"Pity," he said. "Still, I'm in no particular hurry to move. Things have a way of sorting themselves out, I always find."

When they arrived at Chandler's Wharf, Dudley helped her out solicitously. Then, as she turned, imagining that he would escort her as far as her front door, she was dismayed to realize that he had paid off the taxi and it was already driving away.

"Oh, no!" she protested heatedly. "I'm not inviting you in, Dudley. It's far too late."

He laughed softly. "So what? Time never used to matter to you in the old days. One thing I always remember about you is the way you never seemed to get tired."

"These aren't the old days," she snapped. "You can't talk me round, Dudley."

"Aren't you even going to let me come in to call another taxi?"

"Well, I suppose you'll have to now." She relented enough to add, "You can have a cup of coffee while we're waiting."

Once through the front door she told Dudley he'd find the number he needed in her book, then left him to make the call while she went through to the kitchen.

When she emerged with the tray a few minutes later he had drawn the curtains across and was standing by the desk, looking around.

"You've got a nice setup here," he commented approvingly. "Mind you, from what I've been hearing, it will hardly suit you for much longer. You'll need larger premises, with room for all the staff you'll be taking on."

"Heavens, that won't be for ages . . . if ever. Anyway, I'm not sure that I'd ever want to expand beyond having one assistant, or two at the very most. Otherwise, there's a danger of losing the personal touch."

"But the potential is there?" he queried.

"I suppose so. Especially after I've done the Princess Dock job. If all goes well with that, I should be offered more work than I can handle." Natalie glanced at the phone and asked, "How soon did they say your taxi would be here?"

"Er . . . in a few minutes."

But by the time they'd finished the coffee, there was still no sign of a taxi. "You'd better call them again, Dudley," she said.

He looked at her, and said with a coaxing smile, "Let's leave it a little while, my sweet."

"You didn't really phone them at all, did you?" she accused, springing to her feet. "That was a rotten trick."

Dudley was unabashed. "Can you blame me?" He stood up and came toward her, obviously intending to take her in his arms, and he seemed surprised when Natalie put up her hands to fend him off. "I've never forgotten the good times we had, darling, and I was determined to find you again when I came back to this country. Then, when I spotted you in the street this morning, it seemed like an omen that everything was going to work out for us as I've so often dreamed it would."

"Dudley, this is ridiculous," she protested.

He grasped her two hands in his, gazing deep into her eyes. "We've wasted too much time as it is . . . all those empty years! I love you, Natalie, darling . . . I always have and I always will."

"You had a strange way of showing it," she said grimly, snatching her hands away.

"Yes, you're right to reproach me," he conceded. "You were so young, little more than a child, and I was intolerant. You couldn't be expected to understand then that it was *because* I loved you so much that I wanted to show you off to other people in the best possible light. That's why I kept on and on at you, aiming to make you try harder. But I was too harsh, I see that now. I expected far too much from someone of the tender age you were then."

It was something, Natalie told herself ruefully, that Dudley could now admit that he'd been in any way to blame for the failure of their marriage. But he seemed to be blithely ignoring his even more serious fault—the infidelity she'd so cruelly discovered when she'd gone into early labor and given birth to a stillborn child. Well, she was in no mood to remind him and give fresh life to her feelings of bitterness and anger. After so long, it was best if she could draw an obscuring veil over the events leading up to their divorce.

"I'll call for a taxi myself," she said, briskly striding to the telephone.

Dudley gave a heavy sigh of resignation. "If that's how it's got to be, my sweet, I'll go quietly. But I'm giving you fair warning, I'll be back."

When the taxi firm answered, Natalie crisply gave them instructions, and within five minutes the cab arrived. She didn't resist too strongly when Dudley held her shoulders for a good-night kiss, and his lips were warm and ardent on hers.

"Remember the days when we didn't have to say good night?" he murmured huskily.

"They're over, Dudley. Over and done with."

"Don't say that, darling. It sounds too final."

"Divorce *is* final," she pointed out. "You've got to accept that."

"I've been trying to accept it these past years, my sweet, and they were years of hell. Maybe, if I try very hard, I can make a fresh start with you."

"No, it's not possible," she protested wearily.

"Nothing is impossible if you want it enough," he rejoined with a sad, gentle smile. As she opened her mouth to protest once more, he kissed her again quickly, to silence her. Then he was gone, and in a few more moments the sound of the departing taxi was swallowed up in the unceasing murmur of London's nighttime traffic.

Chapter Nine

The next morning, Natalie received a phone call from the Kilmartin Development Corporation. The caller introduced himself as Brian Woodward and said that he'd been instructed by Mr. Kilmartin to let her know whenever the architects were visiting the site at Princess Dock, in case she wished to consult with them. They would, he had just learned, be there today.

Hanging up, Natalie decided that although it would still be some time before her own work commenced in earnest, this was a golden opportunity to sort out one or two points which were not entirely clear to her. So, swiftly changing into a blue denim skirt and jacket, she gathered up her notebook and went straight out to catch a bus.

It was a warm, sunny day that should have been exhilarating; after overnight rain, a fresh breeze had dried the streets and little white puffs of cloud scudded across an azure sky. But Natalie found nothing to enliven her gloomy spirits. Memories of those dark, mocking eyes meeting hers across the dance floor at the Danse Macabre kept returning to torment her. She cursed the day she had first gone to see Grant Kilmartin at his office, thinking it was such a brilliant idea. The profitability of the work she was commissioned to do at Princess Dock, both in cash value and in prestige, couldn't possibly outweigh the heartache involved. But there was no turning back now.

The big corrugated-iron gates at the Princess Dock site were standing open and there were various signs of activity as she walked through. Four cars were drawn up beside the dock basin . . . and one of them, Natalie was dismayed to see, was Grant's dark blue Alfa Romeo. Somehow, she hadn't anticipated that he would be here, too.

She halted, in two minds whether to turn tail and run. While she was dithering, a tall, burly man who wore a construction worker's protective helmet and carried a clipboard hailed her and asked if he could be of assistance.

"I'm Natalie Kent," she began, "and I—"

"Hey! I'm glad to meet you, Mrs. Kent." He extended a large hand and gripped hers firmly. "Nicholas Browne, architect—answers to the name of Nick. Grant showed me your suggestions for this place, and I think they're really great."

He was a pleasant-faced man of about thirty-five, with intelligent, twinkling gray eyes. She soon became so absorbed in talking to him about the plans for Princess Dock that Grant slipped to the back of her mind. Together they went inside the warehouse, where already some of the wooden shuttering had been removed from the windows, allowing light to come flooding in. Two men were busy with measuring equipment, making calculations.

Natalie stopped at one point on the fifth floor and gestured at what was now a solid wall. "I notice that your plans indicate an archway to be cut here, likewise in each of the corner apartments at every level. It would somewhat limit me in my aim to make each dwelling unit unique in character. An arch is rather a distinctive feature, isn't it? Would there be any structural objection to removing the wall completely in some cases, enabling me to use sliding doors, perhaps?"

Nick pursed his lips, considering the point. He riffled

through the sheets on his clipboard, made a mental calculation, then nodded his head.

"I think we could manage that. It would be slightly more expensive, fitting a steel girder to carry the load instead of cutting an arch, but I doubt if we'll have trouble getting Grant to agree to the extra expenditure. He's as impressed with your ideas as I am, and he's not an easy man to please in the ordinary way."

To conceal the betraying flood of color that rushed to her face, Natalie went to a window and gazed out. Voices from below in the yard drew her attention. Grant was there talking to a woman . . . or rather, a girl. To Natalie's shocked surprise, when the girl turned her head and laughed up at him, she saw that it was Jodi Aston.

The color staining Natalie's cheeks drained away in a rush; she felt sickened. By the pool at Hartwell Manor, Grant had been quick to scoff at Blanche Skinner's suggestion that Jodi was starry-eyed about him. But presumably he had since realized that he could turn her youthful infatuation to his advantage. Jodi should be warned about him—not that she'd be likely to listen. Natalie's fists clenched as she fought her sense of despair. Scarcely more than thirty-six hours ago Grant had shared her bed in a night of passionate lovemaking. Then last night he'd been dancing with a glamorous blonde about whom he had obvious intentions. And now, this morning, he was preparing the ground for the seduction of an impressionable young girl in her teens. Was he totally insatiable, obsessed with the need to prove his limitless virility?

"Natalie, are you okay?" Nick Brown had come up behind her, touching her shoulder with concern. Down below, Grant and Jodi were picking their way across the rubble that strewed the yard, his hand gripping her arm to support her. At that instant, as if sensing that he was being watched, Grant turned his head and looked up. Their eyes met and locked, just as in the restaurant last night. Today he did at least acknowledge her, but with the briefest of cool nods. Then he swung away and resumed leading Jodi toward his car.

Natalie forced herself to turn around. "I'm fine, Nick. It was just . . . I felt a bit dizzy for a moment," she finished lamely.

"That kid Grant's with," he said. "I understand she's the daughter of the Mr. Big who's financing this project."

"Yes, that's Jodi Aston. He met her over the weekend at a house party at the Astons' place in Hampshire." Natalie marveled that her voice was so well under control.

Nick gave an admiring laugh. "You've got to hand it to Grant. He's certainly a guy for seizing his opportunities and making the most of them."

Natalie made no comment, feeling sick at heart. With her ears acutely tuned, she heard the familiar throaty sound of Grant's car starting up. Where was he taking Jodi? At least, she consoled herself, their departure meant that she'd be spared a face-to-face encounter with him this morning.

"I think I've got all the information I can handle just now," she told Nick, making her way to the staircase. "When I need more, perhaps I could call you?"

"Sure thing. And we can meet here again sometime." He glanced at his wristwatch. "It's still a bit early for lunch, but would you care to join me for a drink at the Hangman's Noose over the road?"

"No, I . . ." Natalie swallowed, then went on, "Thanks all the same, Nick, but I honestly haven't the time." What she really meant was that she lacked the courage to make bright chat with him in the riverside pub which held so many memories of Grant.

Nick smiled regretfully. "Too bad! Some other time, then?"

"Yes, I'd like that."

The evening stretched ahead emptily. From her front window Natalie had seen Diane setting out with her latest date—a man by the name of Toby Hyatt, who was the new sales manager for a glass firm she dealt with. "He's absolutely dreamy," Diane had declared ecstatically when she'd dropped in that afternoon, a story Natalie had heard so often before. And Riccardo, of course, would as usual be with Maria at the café. Not that she really felt in any mood for company, even if her friends had been available.

Alone, she grew more despondent, more angry, at the thought of Grant and Jodi Aston. What that vulnerable, mixed-up kid needed from her elders was firmness combined with sympathetic understanding, not being taken advantage of by an uncaring Casanova. Why couldn't Grant confine his attentions to the sort of female who knew her way around, like the brazen blonde he'd been with last night? But who am I to be scornful of *her*, Natalie castigated herself, since I too have joined the numerous band of women Grant has bedded? I can never cancel out that fact; and the memory of it, the bliss and the shame of it, will be with me for the rest of my life.

She must try to forget him, banish him from her thoughts. And the way to do that was to keep busy, meet other people . . . anything to keep her mind occupied.

As if in instant answer to her need, a car drove into the courtyard and parked. To her surprise, it was Dudley who got out, and further to her surprise, Natalie realized that she was quite glad to see him.

"I told you I was getting myself some transport," he said cheerfully when she opened the front door to him. "How d'you like it . . . that red one over there?"

"It looks splendid, Dudley. Brand new, isn't it?"

He nodded proudly. "You know me—nothing less than the best."

"What's all *this?*" she asked, indicating the large paper bag he carried, from which protruded the neck of a wine bottle and the end of a crusty French loaf.

"I've brought dinner," he explained, giving her a winning smile. "I thought it would be cozier than eating out again."

"But I didn't agree to have dinner with you tonight," Natalie protested.

"You've got another date?"

"No, but . . ."

Dudley grinned impishly. "I know I'm jumping the gun, darling. But now that I'm here, you aren't going to be so stony-hearted as to send me packing and waste all this good food, are you? There's barbecued spareribs and a mixed salad, with a bottle of rather super rosé. Doesn't that tempt you?"

Natalie hesitated uncertainly, then gave in. "Okay, Dudley, since you're here, and since I hadn't started to prepare anything for myself, you can stay long enough to eat, and I'll share what you've brought. But then I'm going to throw you out, because I've got work to do."

A few minutes later they were both seated at the small table by the window. Dudley poured two glasses of wine, then raised his in a salute.

"To us, Natalie, darling."

To us! Her heart clenched—it was exactly the same toast Grant had used that evening they'd dined on the riverboat. Fiercely she thrust the image from her mind. She would concentrate on what was happening at the present moment, and nothing else.

"I'll drink to *you,* Dudley," she said with a smile, "and you can drink to me."

"Same difference! We're back together again, darling, that's what counts."

She put down her glass very firmly. "No, I told you—"

"Okay, okay," he said pacifically. "I'm sorry. But you can't blame me, my sweet, for trying to hurry along the thing that I most desire in all the world."

As they ate, Dudley talked about his life in New Zealand. Not about his marriage—his second wife wasn't as much as mentioned—but about the places he'd been to and the things he'd done. At one point he mentioned running an agency for the export of Maori craftwork.

"That sounds interesting," Natalie exclaimed. "What sort of things did you deal in?"

"Carving, mostly, in wood and stone, but also some hand-woven fabrics. Some of the Maori work is very fine."

Natalie nodded. "I've seen pictures in magazines, and so on, but never the real thing."

"Well, you'll soon have your chance, darling. I noticed that there's an exhibition of Maori art coming to London next month. I'll take you."

A month seemed an impossibly long time off. Would she still be seeing Dudley then? Suppose, just suppose, she were to allow this revived relationship to continue . . . was it possible that she might discover in him now what she had imagined she'd found in those early days before disillusionment set in? During the years between, she had changed to such an extent that she was almost a different person, and it seemed that Dudley had changed a lot, too. Could it be that, in the light of past mistakes, past unhappiness, they could find a new beginning together?

As if reading her mind, Dudley raised his glass again. "I'm still drinking to *us,* darling, whatever you say. I'm an incurable optimist."

But I could never love Dudley again, no matter what, her heart reminded her. *Even if I can manage to forgive him for the pain and misery he caused me, I could never marry him again. Because now I love Grant.*

"Dudley," she warned, "I don't want you to get any wrong ideas. You forced yourself on me this evening, like you did last night, too. The fact that I've gone along with you to some extent only means that I'm prepared to overlook the past and treat you as an old friend. It doesn't mean—"

He raised a hand to silence her. "The less you say now, my sweet, the less will have to be unsaid when you change your mind."

Natalie sighed, knowing that she ought to put a firm end to this here and now, yet she lacked the energy to cope with a hassle tonight. The shrill ringing of the phone came as a welcome diversion. But her sense of relief was short-lived when she discovered that it was Grant.

"Natalie," he said brusquely, "we must have a talk. I'm coming straight round, and—"

"No," she cut across him. "It . . . it wouldn't be convenient."

"Why not?" he demanded. "Have you someone there with you?"

"As a matter of fact, yes."

"And that someone is a man, I presume?"

The sneer in his voice made Natalie mad. "Correct," she snapped.

"The man you were with last night?"

"You seem to know all the answers," she said in a crisp voice. "Or perhaps you don't."

"What's that supposed to mean?"

"Whatever you feel like making it mean," she countered recklessly, and heard Grant snatch an angry breath.

"Very well," he clipped. "I'll see you tomorrow."

"I'm afraid that won't be convenient, either. Anyway, there'd be no point."

"You seem to be forgetting," he drawled in a tone which carried an underlying threat, "that *I'm* the one who decides whether or not there is any point in our meeting. Be at my office at ten in the morning, Natalie."

"I'll do no such thing."

"Do I read you right?" he queried after a significant pause. "You, the design consultant, are refusing to keep an appointment with the managing director of the development corporation. If you take that sort of attitude, Mrs. Kent, you won't remain in business for long."

She threw an anxious glance in Dudley's direction, but fortunately he seemed absorbed in pouring himself another glass of wine. "That's crazy!" she muttered into the mouthpiece. "You were the one who insisted that business and . . . and other matters should be kept in separate—"

"Are you coming or are you not?" the impatient voice on the line interrupted.

"Suppose I said no?" she retorted wildly.

"I wouldn't really advise that." Grant sounded dangerous, and she had a feeling that he'd stop at nothing to get even with her if she refused his summons.

"Oh . . . if I must. Ten o'clock, you said?"

"I did," he replied curtly, and hung up.

Dudley's eyes were questioning as she rejoined him at the table. "You seemed to be having a spot of trouble there. Who was it?"

Natalie opted for an edited version of the truth. "That was Mr. Kilmartin again. You know, the one who was here when you arrived last night . . . the boss of the firm doing the big conversion job I was telling you about. It's a wretched nuisance, but he wants to see me at his office in the morning. It couldn't be more inconvenient, but . . ." She lifted her shoulders to convey a reluctant bow to the inevitable. ". . . unfortunately, he calls the shots."

Looking thoughtful, Dudley helped himself to a wedge of Camembert cheese. "Does he often interrupt your evenings like this, phoning you or dropping round?"

She pulled a sour face that she hoped was convincing. "Oh, you know what these tycoons are like. They forget about time and just never stop working."

"That's not *my* style," Dudley said with a grin. "What's the purpose of work, if not to provide the means for more interesting pursuits?"

Fortunately, Dudley didn't make too strenuous an objection when, soon after they'd had coffee, she suggested it was time he left. His parting kiss was more intimate and lingering than Natalie wanted, and she pushed herself back, saying with a shaky laugh, "That's enough. Now, get going."

"Until tomorrow," he said softly.

"No, Dudley, I don't think that's a good idea."

He pulled a face at her. "I'll call you anyway. 'Bye for now, darling."

Afterward, as she washed the dishes, she kept thinking about Grant and the shoddy way he was paying her back for last night. He sure was a man who liked to get his revenge! Did it, in fact, explain his relentless pursuit of her even after their furious quarrel? He couldn't tolerate being obligated to her for fixing the financial backing which had rescued his Princess Dock development, and he was determined to exact retribution . . . which was, that she should become totally subjugated to him sexually.

Miserably Natalie felt convinced that she was right, and it reinforced her resolve that never again would she let Grant possess her body. Never, never, never!

Tears squeezed from her eyes and splashed down into the sudsy water.

Diane was on the doorstep early, a tabloid newspaper in her hand, an expression of deep pity in her eyes. "I thought you ought to see this, Natalie."

"What is it?"

Diane held out the paper, which was folded open, and stabbed her finger at a small paragraph. "Read that."

It was a snippet in the Ashley Baxter gossip column: *Spotted at the Danse Macabre the other night, hunky, handsome Grant Kilmartin with lovely socialite Petra Courtney . . . displaying oodles of fond togetherness. Seems like they've turned the thermostat from "cool" right back to "high heat."*

"Best that you know," Diane muttered grimly.

Natalie felt waves of pain beat through her, but she managed a defiant shrug. "I did know. I happened to be at the Danse Macabre that same night, and saw them. It's no big deal."

"No big deal? But I thought that you and he—"

"He and I nothing. Like I told you, it's just a professional connection."

"Oh, Natalie, why pretend? You forget that I know he spent the night here with you."

"And that's supposed to rock the universe?" she flashed, injecting worldly scorn into her voice. "It's something that's never happened to *you*, of course."

"With me it's different," Diane said impatiently. "But you're not the sort to go in for casual sex. Nor would I be," she added with a rueful grin, "if I could find the other kind."

"Honestly," Natalie insisted, "you're getting your lines crossed, Di. I shan't be shedding any tears over Grant Kilmartin."

"If you say so." But the sympathetic look on Diane's face told Natalie that she wasn't convinced. "Anyway," she went on curiously, "how come you were eating at a swish place like the Danse Macabre?"

"Oh . . . someone took me."

"Someone? Don't be maddening . . . level with me."

Natalie decided it would have to come out sometime. And maybe this would get Diane off the Grant track. "As a matter of fact, it was Dudley, my ex-husband."

"Your ex . . . ?" Diane's expression changed to blank astonishment. "But how come? What's this all about?"

"That's no big deal, either. Dudley's back in England, and he and I happened to run into each other in the street. We chatted and he asked me out to dinner."

"He has to be doing darned well," Diane commented, looking impressed. "Taking you to just about the priciest restaurant there is."

"He certainly doesn't seem short of money," Natalie said neutrally.

"So where's it heading? Are you seeing him again?"

"As a matter of fact, he came here to eat last night."

"My word, he is keen! Does he want you two to get back together?"

Natalie looked at her friend helplessly. "I rather think he does."

"And?"

"No way, Di. When we split up, we parted on the worst possible terms. It's not something I can forget."

Diane looked thoughtful. "I could say the same about my ex. But if he was to reappear now and show that much interest in me . . . well, I'm none too sure that I wouldn't grab him thankfully. One thing the past few years have taught me, Natalie, is that better men than Richard—for all his faults—don't grow on trees."

* * *

Deliberately Natalie was a few minutes after ten arriving at Grant's office. A tiny enough act of defiance, but it did something for her battered pride.

"You're five minutes late," he snapped, indicating the digital clock on the wall.

"You shouldn't have waited," she countered sarcastically. "I wouldn't have minded in the least if you'd gone out."

He glared at her impatiently. "It seems that making an appointment at my office is the only way I can be honored with your company."

"This is the only place we have any reason to meet," she said. "Here, or maybe at the site."

Grant considered her in silence for a few moments, both of them still standing. He seemed, for the first time since she'd known him, a bit at a loss. Then his voice grated against the silence. "I'd like to know just what kind of game you're playing, Natalie. Businesswise, I can understand your tactics. Having fixed it so that I was forced to accept you as the Princess Dock design consultant, you've made sure I shall be forever looking over my shoulder to watch that you don't pull another fast trick. It must give you an intoxicating sense of power over me. But even that isn't enough for you, seemingly. You have to go and rub salt into my wounds."

"Pure rubbish from start to finish," she flared.

"Not from my viewpoint. You aren't the usual sort of teasing female, are you, Natalie? The sort who strings a man along for all she's worth, then suddenly leaves him high and dry? No, you're far more devilishly subtle than that. After an award-winning display of reluctance, you eventually appear to succumb, but you only allow the poor dope one single taste of paradise. Then you give him the brush-off, laughing yourself silly at the thought of what he's suffering."

Goaded, Natalie threw back at him heatedly, "You

seem to have solaced yourself in double-quick time. First with Petra Courtney, and then with Jodi Aston. You don't have any scruples at all, do you, leading a young girl like Jodi astray."

Grant's head jerked up, and his eyes spat fire. Then, shrugging his broad shoulders, he remarked with a sneer, "I can't believe you're human enough to feel jealous. So it must mean you're livid at the thought of my finding consolation instead of burning in a hell of frustration."

Hating him, Natalie said hoarsely, "If that's all you brought me here to say, I'm going right now."

As she turned toward the door, Grant quickly moved around his desk and caught her roughly by the arm. His touch seared like a branding iron. "You'll stay right here until I say you can leave, and I haven't finished with you yet." Abruptly he let go of her and curbed his anger. The loathsome sneer was back in his voice as he continued, "So now you're giving another poor fool the Natalie Kent treatment. How long will it be, I ask myself, before *he* discovers that he'll be allowed to enter the gates of heaven just once, then be cast aside to suffer the torment of the damned? Perhaps it would be a kindness for me to give him a friendly warning."

"Don't you dare interfere!"

Grant's lips curled in grim satisfaction. "That scared you, didn't it? I doubt if he'd listen, though, even if I were to take the trouble to warn him. He'll be totally hooked by now, for sure."

"You're completely wrong about Dudley."

"So his name is Dudley. Dudley . . . what?"

"If you really want to know," she said with a cool, straight look, "it's Kent. Dudley is my ex-husband."

Grant became very still and his face drained of color. At last he muttered, "You told me that he was living in New Zealand."

"He was. But now he's come back."

"I gathered from what you said—always assuming you weren't lying—that he treated you so badly that you were compelled to walk out on him. Yet now he's bringing you flowers, taking you out to dinner, spending a cozy evening at your studio. What's going on, Natalie? Is it romance time come round again?"

About to deny that there was anything more between herself and Dudley beyond simply the renewal of their acquaintanceship, Natalie hesitated. It might be better to leave Grant with a rather different impression.

"A lot of water has gone under the bridge since our marriage broke up," she said with a little shrug, "and we've both mellowed a bit. Anyway, I see no reason why Dudley and I should be condemned to remain enemies. It's much better to get things into a common-sense perspective."

Grant was studying her face intently, as if searching for a truth she hadn't yet revealed. "And what, exactly, is a common-sense perspective in this case?"

While Natalie was gesturing vaguely in reply, allowing him to believe as much or as little as he chose, there was a sudden commotion in the secretary's office outside. Then the door burst open and a woman entered. To her dismay, Natalie recognized her as the blonde who'd been with Grant at the Danse Macabre—Petra Courtney, as she now knew. She was wearing a pale green skirt and jacket in butter-soft suede that must have cost a fortune.

"Grant, darling, that dragon of a secretary of yours tried to tell me that you were too busy to see me, but I slipped past her." She went to him and laid her hands on his chest, standing on tiptoe and touching his cheek with her lips in a fond greeting. Then, as if catching sight of Natalie for the first time, she arched her fine-drawn eyebrows interrogatively.

Grant, looking totally unruffled, introduced them.

"This is Mrs. Natalie Kent, who's to be the design consultant on that Princess Dock project of mine. This," he said to Natalie, "is Miss Petra Courtney."

As if I didn't know, thought Natalie bitterly. Petra, who'd barely even noticed her, said brightly, "Darling, I'm sure that Mrs. Kent can come back some other time. Daddy is making up a party for the races, and I've come to carry you off."

He shook his head. "Sorry, Petra, but I'm afraid I'm far too busy."

She pouted prettily. "I should have remembered how seriously you always take your work, darling. Never mind, we can see each other this evening instead. Sally Frencham called while I was having breakfast about one of those fabulous parties of hers. I told her I'd bring you along." She giggled. "It will be something else for that wicked Ashley Baxter to put in his column. I suppose you saw the bit about us this morning?"

Grant nodded, his expression giving nothing away. "I wonder who primed Ashley Baxter. Was it you, by any chance?"

Petra gurgled again. "I might have given him just the teensiest little hint, darling." She sighed extravagantly. "Well, if I really can't persuade you to forget work for once and have a lovely day out, I suppose I'd better be going. Daddy's waiting downstairs in the Rolls, and I don't want him getting into one of his fearful rages."

Natalie, not trusting herself to be left alone with Grant again after this scene, decided to beat a hasty retreat. "I'll be off too," she murmured, heading for the door.

"No, wait," Grant rasped. "I still haven't finished with you, Natalie."

She turned, and managed to meet his gaze unflinchingly. "I rather thought we'd covered the ground already, Mr. Kilmartin."

Grant hesitated. Petra was glancing from one to the

other of them, gauging the situation. Then he said abruptly, "On second thought, I'll leave things there. I'll be letting you know when I require to see you again."

He had succeeded, Natalie realized, in turning the tables and making her escape seem like a peremptory dismissal. With all the dignity she could dredge up, she walked briskly from his office and even managed a smile for his secretary as she passed through the small outer room. Descending in the elevator felt like dropping into a void, a void as empty as her future life.

Chapter Ten

When Natalie arrived home, there was a message from Dudley on her answering machine. He'd called to say that a Birmingham firm he'd mentioned to her last night had asked to see him, and he would be driving up there right away. "Sorry it means that I won't be seeing you tonight, darling," he finished, "but I'll be back tomorrow and I'll see you then."

She'd forgotten all about Dudley calling to make a date, and she was grateful for the respite his message gave her. Today she felt too emotionally fragile to parry her ex-husband's hustling attempt to get close to her again. By tomorrow, she hoped, she'd be in a calmer frame of mind.

It was a vain hope. A long, restless night left her feeling limp and dejected. She had no appetite for breakfast, and no zest for work. Forcing herself to sit at the drawing board, she did little else than doodle for an hour or more. Then, glancing up vaguely for inspiration, she spotted a damp patch on the ceiling just to the right of the sofa.

Rising to her feet, she went to inspect it more closely. It wasn't raining and hadn't been for two days, so something must have sprung a leak. Even as she watched, the patch seemed to grow a little; a bead of moisture formed, and dropped to the carpet. Hastily fetching a bowl to collect any further drips, she pondered whether she'd better call a plumber at once, or hope that it would soon stop of its own accord. Maybe Riccardo, if he was in, could advise what she ought to do.

While she hesitated, someone knocked at her door. She opened up to find Dudley standing there, looking very pleased with himself.

"Hi, darling. I'm just back and I thought I'd look in on you before going to the hotel, to see what's on our agenda for today." He came walking in, and gave her a fond kiss. "How about us having lunch together, and I can tell you all about my good news? I landed the agency okay."

"I'm so glad for you, Dudley."

He smiled at her tenderly. "I really think you are, Natalie. So why the worried frown?"

"I've got a problem," she said ruefully, and pointed to the damp patch. "I don't know how long it's been there, but I've only just noticed it. Should I call a plumber, do you think?"

"Spoken like a woman who's not used to having a man about the house," Dudley commented with a grin. He slipped off his jacket and began rolling up his shirtsleeves. "Now, then, where's the trapdoor to the crawl space?"

"But I didn't mean for you to go up there," she protested.

"Don't you think I'm capable?" he teased.

"It's not that. It just doesn't seem fair to ask you to cope with something like this."

"I'm *volunteering*," he said firmly.

"Well, thanks, if you're sure you don't mind. The trapdoor is in the lobby by the bathroom, and there's a stepladder in the cupboard. Oh, and I've got a flashlight somewhere."

"Leave it to me, then. I'll just go and fetch a few tools from my car."

Dudley was up in the loft space for about fifteen minutes, during which time Natalie heard vague clanking noises. Then his head reappeared at the trapdoor, and he was grinning triumphantly.

"It was just a joint that needed tightening," he explained as he came down the ladder and closed the trap. "Everything's okay now. I doubt if that patch on the ceiling will really show when it's dried out."

"That's great!" Natalie said, vastly relieved. "But, Dudley, you're absolutely filthy . . . your shirt and your hair and everything. It must be really grimy up there."

He glanced down at himself and pulled a rueful face. "I'd better see what I can do to clean up. Okay for me to take a shower?"

"Of course. And if you put your things outside the door, I'll give your trousers a brush and rinse your shirt through. It'll be dry in no time in the dryer."

"Thanks, darling. If I'd had any sense, I'd have taken my shirt off before going up there, but I didn't think of it."

Dudley went off to the bathroom, and a couple of minutes later Natalie found his clothes dumped outside the door. She could hear him humming cheerfully to himself under the shower. His shirt she washed through by hand at the kitchen sink, then popped it into the tumble dryer; his trousers, fortunately, were soon put right by a vigorous brushing. Then she applied herself to making coffee. When she heard a knock at the front door, she went to answer it distractedly, wondering whether to accept Dudley's invitation to lunch. She supposed she owed him that now, in view of his helpfulness.

Opening the door, she stepped back with a gasp of dismay. It was Grant.

"I've come," he said grimly, "to finish what I didn't get around to saying yesterday at my office." Without

an invitation, he strode past her into the studio. Natalie
closed the door, then turned to remonstrate with him.
But the expression in Grant's eyes checked her. He
looked angry, bitter, contemptuous—all those things.
But there was something else, too. Almost, it seemed
to her, a kind of pleading. "Things have somehow gone
crazily wrong," he went on in a subdued voice. "We've
both said some pretty ugly things to one another."

She swallowed down a lump in her throat. "It's
cleared the air between us, Grant. We know now
exactly how we stand. We're merely associates in the
Princess Dock development, and nothing more."

"Not true, Natalie. When something momentous
happens between a man and a woman the way it did
with us, it can't be just struck from the record. You and
I spent an unforgettable night together in your bedroom here. A wonderful night."

"It was good on a certain level," she agreed huskily.

"On the only level that counts," he retorted.

"To you, perhaps. But as for me, Grant . . . I'm not
looking for cheap thrills."

His dark eyes flickered. "There was nothing cheap
about it. When the chemistry really works for two
people, a kind of magic takes over. We both recognized
it that night."

"Am I supposed to be flattered?" she asked sarcastically. "No doubt it's quite an honor to be high-rated by
a man as experienced as you. What score, I wonder, did
you award me on the Grant Kilmartin scale? Eight out
of ten . . . or do I overrate myself?"

"Stop that!" he commanded, his face flaming with
anger. Then he made a visible effort to gain control of
himself. In a voice that was almost humble, he said, "If
you really want to know, Natalie, it's never, ever been
so good for me before. No other woman has carried me
to the highest peaks of ecstasy as you did."

Natalie's heart cried out in pain as she looked at him.

She loved this man . . . against all reason, against all common sense, against her own self-interest. The longing for him, the burning need she felt for him, sprang from that love. Her eager response to his passion couldn't have happened without love. And all Grant offered her in return was the testimonial that she had surpassed every other candidate in satisfying his sexual need. *The only level that counts,* he'd said cynically.

"Please go away," she whispered on a thin thread of breath.

"You don't really want me to go away," he insisted, his eyes on her face. "I think I read you better than you read yourself. It might suit your vanity . . . feed your sense of power, to lead me on, accept me just once, then give me the brush-off. But you're hurting yourself as much as you're hurting me, Natalie. You can try to outstare me now, but you know damn well that I'd only have to touch you, just lay one finger on you, and you'd melt in my arms again, as you always do."

"You're wrong," she said fiercely. "Not anymore."

"No?" His dark gaze ran over her slowly, lingeringly, as if peeling off her clothes to savor again the body he knew in such intimate detail. It felt to Natalie almost as though he were actually caressing her, stroking her naked breasts, her stomach, the sensitive skin of her inner thighs. Standing before him, she began to tremble, and her face and neck were flushing with hot color.

"Natalie . . . chuck me my trousers, will you, darling."

The unexpected voice caused them both to jerk around. In her tense absorption with Grant she had completely forgotten about Dudley. He emerged from the lobby with nothing on except for a towel gripped around his middle. Noticing Grant, he added with an apologetic grin, "Sorry, I didn't realize anyone was here."

"That's obvious!" Grant's voice was like a whiplash

and his scorn cut her to the bone. "I had no idea,
Natalie, that things were so far advanced along the road
to your reunion. Is the happy day fixed, or are you not
bothering this time around to make things quite so . . .
conventional?"

Dudley chuckled easily, looking a confident man.
"Natalie knows how I feel. Nothing would make me
happier than to become her husband again."

"Then I hope you appreciate what you'll be taking
on. Natalie has become an extremely tough, astute
businesswoman these days, and she's going all-out to
make a big impact in her career. Does that thought
appeal to you?"

Dudley, not smiling anymore, answered his scathing
remarks steadily. "I love Natalie . . . I always have and
I always will. I hope to win back her love, too. That's
all I ask for, all I'll ever want."

Grant's fists were clenched into two hard balls, and
his face was dark with suppressed fury. But the carefully level tone of his voice made its cutting edge all the
sharper. "I wish you luck, Mr. Kent. You'll need it!"

With that, Grant was gone, slamming the door with a
violence that rattled the windows. There was a certain
smug satisfaction in Dudley's expression which belied
his words. "Damned cheek of the man. I had half a
mind to punch him on the nose."

"No," Natalie said with a shudder. "I wouldn't want
that sort of scene." How much had Dudley overheard?
she wondered miserably. Enough, almost certainly, to
give him an accurate picture of her relationship with
Grant . . . that they had slept together. Why, though,
should she feel so deeply embarrassed? Dudley wasn't
her husband anymore, she owed him no fidelity. "Er
. . . your shirt should be dry by now," she stammered,
and dived into the kitchen to take it out of the dryer.

When Dudley reemerged from the bathroom, fully

dressed, he commented, "What a heel that chap Kilmartin is, talking about you like that!" He looked at her sharply. "Will this quarrel put paid to that big job you were telling me about?"

"You mean Princess Dock? No, that's all tied up by contract. He's committed to it the same way I am."

"That's just as well," he said with a nod of satisfaction. "Kilmartin looks to me the sort of mean-spirited guy who would go out of his way to get his revenge."

"Get his revenge?" she echoed dazedly. "How do you mean?"

Dudley came and laid a hand on her shoulder in a gesture of sympathy. "Listen, darling . . . don't let's pretend with one another, eh? It's obvious to me that you and he . . . well, you had something going between you, but that you've now given him his marching orders. Any decent man would accept that, but he lookes the type to be vindictive. My guess is that he would dearly like to hit back by taking that nice fat contract away from you, but luckily you say he can't do that."

"I don't believe he would, anyway," she whispered, then wondered why she'd said it. How much could she really put her trust in Grant's oft-repeated insistence that, with him, personal and working relationships were things entirely apart?

"I wouldn't care for you to have to rely on Kilmartin's good nature," Dudley remarked sagely. "I'd say it's a case of 'hell hath no fury' in reverse."

"You're making too much of it all," she muttered unhappily. "It . . . it only happened once, and I was sorry afterward." Then, because she wanted to impress on Dudley that she wasn't a cheap and easy conquest for men, she added, "As a matter of fact, that was the one and only time since you and I split up."

"You poor angel," he said with a gentle smile.

"Honestly, a type like that deserves to be shot, taking advantage of your trusting nature and your loneliness and everything."

Taking advantage, Natalie thought forlornly, of her *love*. But Grant wouldn't have been aware of that fact. How would he have acted if he had been? Would he still have pursued her as relentlessly, or would fear of becoming entrapped have made him hesitate? The question was academic now, anyway. He would never want to come back—and she would never accept him back. The split between them was doubly positive. She should be glad, she told herself, but instead she felt only an empty, aching misery.

"Hey!" said Dudley. "You badly need cheering up, darling. So how about that lunch date you promised me? Where shall we go?"

"I haven't promised to have lunch with you," Natalie pointed out.

"Then I'll claim your company as my reward for the plumbing job."

She nodded reluctantly, knowing that it would be churlish to refuse. "Okay. But I can't spare much time, so it'll have to be a bar snack at the pub across the road."

"Anything you say," he agreed.

In the ornate Victorian pub, they drank beer from glass tankards and each consumed a plateful of savory-tasting lasagne. Dudley told her about the agency arrangement he'd fixed up in Birmingham, for which he had great hopes.

"I'm very happy for you," Natalie said sincerely.

"And I'm happy if you're happy," he replied with a quick smile. "It's as simple as that."

She refused to allow Dudley to come back to the studio with her, waving him good-bye from the court-yard as he drove off in his new car. He'd tried hard to make plans for another meeting, but she wouldn't be pinned down and had been vaguely discouraging. She just felt too drained to be more definite and final with him at the moment.

The following morning brought Natalie an unexpected visitor. "Why, Lady Aston, how nice!" she exclaimed. "Do come in."

"Thank you, my dear. I've just been to see your friend Mrs. Fielding about some of her glassware as a wedding present for my husband's niece. She does such beautiful work, it was difficult to make up my mind, but I finally chose a set of crystal goblets with a matching decanter."

"I'm so glad you found something suitable." Natalie was delighted that her bright idea had paid off and that Diane had picked up a nice order as a result. Hastily plumping up the sofa cushions, she invited Celia to sit down. "Would you like some coffee, Lady Aston?"

"That would be lovely," she said. "I hope it's not inconvenient, my dropping in like this, but I thought as I was so near . . . To be truthful, I wanted the chance to see your studio properly. It looked so charming that day I called to collect you in the car." She glanced around her with lively interest. "Although you've used a number of clever modern ideas, you've still managed to retain a homey feeling. I do like that Spanish rug, by the way. Oh, and what a beautiful bergère chair."

A few minutes later, over their coffee, Celia asked how Princess Dock was progressing.

"It's still too early for me to do more than formulate a few general plans," Natalie told her. "I've had a thought for the penthouse which I think you'll approve of. There's a lovely early-Victorian carved-oak fireplace at a big house in Cambridge that's to be demolished, and I'd like to put in a bid. I have a photograph of it to show you. I think that the fireplace would make the ideal focal point to give real meaning to the living room." She fetched the photo which a Cambridge dealer had sent her, and Lady Aston exclaimed with delight. "Most impressive! I always say there's nothing like a good open fire on a winter evening."

"So shall I make an offer for it?"

"Yes, please, dear."

"It will be quite expensive, I'm afraid. This sort of item is hard to come by."

Celia waved aside the question of expense, as Natalie had known she would. The more he had to pay for something, the better Sir Matthew was pleased. They discussed various other ideas of Natalie's; then Celia said, "I expect, dear, I shall be seeing you next Tuesday at the opening ceremony of our new shopping arcade?"

"At Maida Vale, you mean? No, I haven't had any hand in that project."

"But I thought . . . won't Mr. Kilmartin be bringing you?"

"No." The single word of denial sounded too abrupt, and Natalie hastened to embellish it. "There really wouldn't be any point, Lady Aston. It's like I've been telling you all along . . . Grant Kilmartin and I are just business associates, that's all."

Celia Aston released her disappointment in a long sigh. "I suppose I'm a silly, sentimental woman, but I really was hoping that you two might make a match of it. Seeing you together, I thought you looked an ideal couple. I can't imagine two people better suited to one another."

Natalie turned her head away to hide her rising color. Celia Aston's primly conventional mind would be shocked to the core to know just how well suited she and Grant had been in one particular respect. This was a potentially dangerous conversation and she'd be giving herself away if she didn't tread with caution.

"Still, if it's not to be," Celia tutted unhappily, "then it's no use my bemoaning the fact. But I find it so distressing to see you letting your life drift away, Natalie. Oh, I know how women of your generation think in terms of total equality, and I applaud your insistence on the right to make a career for yourself. But nothing alters the fact, my dear, that a woman is incomplete without a man. It's such a pity that your broken marriage has left you with such bitter feelings against the whole male sex."

Natalie was silent for a moment and then said, "As a matter of fact, Lady Aston, I bumped into my ex-husband in the street the other day. It was odd, but I found that a lot of the old bitterness had gone."

Lady Aston looked at her interestedly, then put down her coffee cup before asking, "What is he doing in this country? Is he here on vacation? Or business?"

"He's returned to live permanently." Foreseeing the next question, Natalie added, "Actually, he's divorced again."

"He doesn't appear to have a very good record in that respect," Celia remarked with a frown.

"From what he told me, I rather think it wasn't his fault this time. At least, not to the same degree." She toyed with her spoon absently. "Dudley has changed, Lady Aston."

"In what way, dear?"

"Oh . . . he's softer, more easygoing than he was. More like the Dudley I first met, before . . ." Natalie shrugged. "I suppose I've mellowed a lot, too."

"I can't say, my dear, not knowing you until recently. But this I do know—that you would be a fine catch for any man. Tell me," Celia probed gently, "are you contemplating a reconciliation?"

Natalie shook her head. "Nothing like that. It's just that . . . well, we've sort of made friends again."

Celia was pensive, then said, "I have a little idea. Why don't you bring Dudley to the opening of the shopping arcade?"

"Oh, no, I couldn't do that." Unthinkable, because Grant would be there, the leading figure of the occasion.

"But why not, my dear? It will only be for an hour or so, and afterward I'm inviting some of the people concerned back to our apartment for tea. Do come. I would so much like to meet Dudley."

Natalie smiled, sidestepping a definite refusal. "It's nice of you to invite us, Lady Aston, but I very much doubt if Dudley would be free on a weekday afternoon. He's very busy at the moment."

"We'll leave it open, then, but do both of you come if you can. I've also asked that nice friend of yours, Mrs. Fielding. There are a couple of craft shops in the arcade, and I thought an introduction to them might result in some extra business for her."

"You really are a kindhearted person, Lady Aston. Always ready to offer a helping hand to other people."

Natalie was awarded a gratified smile. "Perhaps it's because I have so much of the world's goods myself, my dear . . . more than my fair share. I'd feel guilty if I didn't try to do what little I can for others." The smile faded and Celia looked somber. "I have a great deal to be grateful for, despite the sadness of losing dear Keith. I'd be a very contented woman, except that . . ."

Except that her daughter was being willfully difficult, Natalie finished for her silently. But, feeling a coward, she refrained from asking about Jodi. Another time she would try to repay Celia Aston's kindnesses by lending a sympathetic ear. But just at this moment her emotions were in too fragile a state for her to be much good at listening to other people's troubles.

Dudley phoned on Saturday morning to ask her to have dinner with him that evening, but Natalie refused on the pretext of some urgent work. On Sunday he called again "just for a little chat." She quickly invented a client she had to see, who was only in town over the weekend, saying, "I'm getting ready to go out right now, Dudley, and I won't be back till late."

It was a vain hope that he'd gotten the message that she didn't want to see him again. On Monday, when he phoned, he said, "Listen, darling, I have to go and see a man in Brighton tomorrow. Why not come with me? It would do you the world of good to have a nice day by the sea."

"No . . . it's quite impossible." She had a genuine way out this time. "My client, Lady Aston, has invited me to the opening of a new shopping arcade near her home in Maida Vale."

"That sounds interesting," Dudley exclaimed quickly. "How about me coming along with you?"

"You have an appointment in Brighton," she reminded him crisply.

"Oh, I can easily make that another day. I'd much rather come to this thing with you."

Natalie started to tell him that it was out of the question. But then she hesitated. Why not take Dudley along and let Grant see how little she cared what he chose to think about her? It would demonstrate once and for all her total indifference to his opinion.

"As a matter of fact," she said slowly, "Lady Aston did say that I could bring you along with me if I cared to."

"Oh?" Dudley sounded smugly pleased. "What were you telling her about me?"

"Nothing much," she said hastily. "I just happened to mention that I'd met up with my ex-husband again. So if you really want to come, Dudley, then you might as well. It's at two o'clock, so I'll expect you here a bit before that. Okay?"

He arrived next day looking very spruce in a new dark gray pinstripe suit. Evading his attempted kiss, she said lightly, "I can't think why you're so keen to

come to this 'do.' It won't be anything much. You'd
have done better to stick to your original arrangement
and gone to Brighton.''

"It was a chance to be with you, darling, and I wasn't
going to pass that up. Don't worry, I won't lose out by
it. I'm riding high at the moment, and that's how I plan
to stay. I've got more ideas in this head of mine than I'll
ever be able to put into practice, and every one of
them's a winner.'' With a wave of his hand he dismissed
the subject. "You look absolutely stunning, a real
knockout. You'll turn all the other women green with
envy.''

Natalie had taken enormous pains with her appearance this afternoon. It was important to her act of
defiance against Grant that she really look her best. She
wore a very feminine lawn dress in a pale almond green
and her hair, brushed to a gleaming silkiness, was tied
back with a chiffon scarf of the same color. At the very
last moment she'd fastened her mother's sapphire-and-
diamond pin at her shoulder—the only piece of really
valuable jewelry she possessed.

"Well, I'm ready," she told him. "I'll go across the
courtyard and give my friend Diane a shout. You don't
mind that I asked her to come in the car with us? It
would've seemed silly for her to take a bus.''

"Of course I don't mind, darling," Dudley assured
her, beaming. "Any friend of yours is a friend of mine,
you know that.''

Diane, wearing a cherry-colored linen suit, was
ready and waiting for them at her front door. Natalie
made the introductions, and while getting into the car,
Diane found the chance to whisper, "I thoroughly
approve. In fact, you'd better watch out, or I might try
to steal him from you.''

Scarcely more than fifteen minutes later Dudley
swung the car down the ramp to the new underground
car park at the shopping arcade. Against her will,

Natalie was much impressed by what Grant had achieved here. It was a spacious glass-roofed enclosure with cool greenery and splashing fountains and a number of places to sit and rest. The little shops were each individual and unique, yet there was a skillful unity of design which tied them together. Crowds of people were milling around, and sherry was being proffered by white-jacketed stewards. Celia Aston had persuaded her husband to grace the function with his presence, and the two of them were much in evidence as local VIP's. But Natalie couldn't see Grant anywhere, and wondered where he was. She felt impatient to watch the expression on his face when he saw her here with Dudley.

A shining black Rolls-Royce drew up at the entrance to the arcade, and to a flurry of applause and clicking cameras a man in full mayoral regalia descended. He was followed by Grant, an immaculate, impressive figure in a charcoal-gray suit. And with him was Petra Courtney, wearing a fabulous black-and-white outfit and heels a mile high. Sick with a feeling of helpless jealousy, Natalie watched as the three of them crossed to a low wooden podium and seated themselves. A short, rather fussy man, who announced himself as the chairman of the local Chamber of Trade, called for silence and introduced Mr. Grant Kilmartin. Grant rose to his feet and primed his audience by making a joke that got everyone laughing. For just a moment he seemed to falter when his dark gaze came to rest on Natalie. Then, without a flicker of recognition, he continued speaking in a more serious vein, giving credit to the farsightedness of the various traders concerned, the ready assistance of the local planning officials, and the forbearance of local residents who'd had to suffer a lot of inconvenience these past months. He hoped they would now feel that it had all been worthwhile.

"And now," he finished, "it gives me great pleasure

to invite his worship the mayor to declare this arcade open."

Natalie hardly noticed the ceremonial that followed. She was suddenly wishing desperately that she'd not let Celia Aston persuade her to come this afternoon. How could she have thought to score off Grant by letting him see her escorted by Dudley? Grant was totally indifferent to her now, uncaring what she did, or with whom. More than once Petra's green eyes glittered triumphantly in Natalie's direction, but Natalie looked back stonily.

When the official proceedings were over, those invited to the Astons' began an exodus to the mansion block across the street. By the time Natalie and Dudley arrived, Celia's large drawing room was packed with people, all talking hard and being served tea and fancy cakes by a bevy of hired waitresses. Celia came forward and greeted them warmly, laying a hand on Natalie's arm.

"I've been longing to be introduced to your Dudley," she said eagerly, "but there wasn't an opportunity in all that melee. Not that it's much less crowded up here, I'm afraid. So this is that handsome ex-husband of yours!" She smiled at Dudley approvingly. "Natalie told me about your chance meeting the other day."

"Was it really chance, Lady Aston?" His voice was half-joking, half-serious. "That's what I keep asking myself. Somehow it seems more like the hand of fate."

Celia gave him a straight, challenging look. "Natalie is a very brave young woman, you know. She's not had an easy life, but she's fought through and come out on top, all due to her own initiative and hard work. She deserves some good things to happen to her now, Mr. Kent."

He met Celia's gaze steadily. "I hope that *I'm* a good thing for her, Lady Aston. Believe me, I'm going to try to be. We all make mistakes, but not everyone is lucky enough to have the chance to put his mistakes right. I'm not about to throw that chance away."

"Good!" Celia's total approval of him was plain. "Now, come and meet some of the other people."

Later, Natalie and Dudley became separated. She could see him across the room, engaged in earnest conversation with Sir Matthew. Diane, who was standing by the fireplace, gave her a wave and led over a thin, quiet-looking man in his late thirties.

"Jeremy Stanbury . . . Natalie Kent, my neighbor at Chandler's Wharf," she introduced. "Jeremy is a sculptor, Natalie, but he also owns a super craft shop in the arcade, so I'm hoping we might be able to do some business together." From the animation in her friend's face, Natalie guessed that she was hoping for more than just business. Jeremy Stanbury was quite unlike Diane's usual choice of man, though. There was a reserved air of refinement about him, but his gray eyes were warm as he looked at Diane. Perhaps, Natalie thought hopefully, it augured well for a blossoming relationship that would prove to be more enduring than her usual brief, hectic affairs.

"Uh-uh—look who's here!" Diane nodded her head across the room to where Grant and Petra were in laughing conversation with a man in a bow tie who wore his fair hair down to his shoulders and had rather an affected manner. "That," she said significantly, "is Ashley Baxter, the gossip columnist. Those two don't seem to be resenting that sly paragraph he wrote about them the other day. What will his next choice tidbit be about them, I wonder."

Perhaps it was the sherry Natalie had drunk earlier, plus the heat of the crowded room, but she suddenly wanted some fresh air. Leaving Diane and Jeremy, she slipped out through the open French windows to the balcony. There were several other people out here, having had the same idea. Natalie exchanged a few pleasantries with them; then she moved along to Lady Aston's small conservatory, the nearest thing Celia could get to having a garden at this town apartment. Under the glass the air was warm and humid, but at least it offered Natalie solitude. She felt a desperate need for a few minutes alone to get a grip on her fraying nerves. It had been a stupid mistake to come here this afternoon and expose herself to the pain of seeing Grant with Petra Courtney.

She was standing fingering the fleshy leaves of some bright green succulent plant when a footstep behind her made her wheel around. To her horror it was Grant, his tall, leanly muscled figure seeming even more dauntingly overpowering as he stepped into the confined space.

"Hiding yourself away, Natalie?" he asked with a sardonic smile, though the look in his eyes was deadly.

"I . . . I just wanted a breath of air."

"In *here?*" he queried mockingly.

"I mean . . . well, it's quiet, and . . ."

"Surely you can't already be finding the company of your newest lover such a bore?"

She bit her lip. "Dudley is not my lover."

"No?" Grant's teeth gleamed whitely as he gave her a wolflike smile. "Still, I suppose that 'lover' is something of a misnomer for a man who used to be your husband. He seems to be resuming the role—in his behavior, if not by title."

"You're talking nonsense," she said hotly.

"So, the other day, he'd just dropped in for a chat about old times, had he?" Grant's tone was thick with sarcasm. "In such circumstances one would expect him to take all his clothes off."

Natalie flushed. "There's a simple explanation for Dudley's being undressed."

"I'm sure there is," he said snidely. "Perhaps he was feeling the heat. It was, as I recall, quite a warm day."

"As a matter of fact . . ." she began, then stopped.

Why should she give Grant the satisfaction of having her rush to explain? Let him think what he liked about her and Dudley. "As a matter of fact," she amended, "it's no business of yours!"

Grant stood there blocking her only means of escape, his fists thrust into his hips. To get out she would have to push her way past him. The thought of making actual physical contact with his warm, vibrant flesh sent shivers of apprehension through her.

"If . . . if you don't mind, Grant, I'd like to return to the drawing room now."

He didn't budge. "But I do mind. You were showing no sign of wanting to return when I found you here. Surely my presence can't be so obnoxious?"

"Dudley will be wondering where I am," she faltered.

"He should have kept a closer eye on you," Grant said with an unpleasant little smile. "He'll find he needs to, poor chump, if he's really intent on tying the knot with you again. From what I've seen, I can't imagine you taking the marriage vows very seriously, Natalie."

Grant's venom and the unfairness of his accusations made her want to cry foolish tears. Choking them back, she gave him a look that was as flint-hard as his own. "Shouldn't you be getting back to Petra?" she inquired meaningfully.

"All in good time."

"How chivalrous," she mocked. "Do your bedmates get to expect that sort of cavalier treatment?"

"You didn't stick around long enough to find out, did you?" he threw back carelessly.

Natalie gasped under the whiplash cruelty of his tongue. "You . . . you're despicable," she cried. "Now, let me get by."

She started forward, desperation making her determined to force her way past him. But Grant caught her wrist in a steel grip and dragged her around to face him.

His slate-gray eyes were blazing with anger. "You can't wait to get back to your nasty little game, can you?" he grated.

Natalie tried to drag herself free, but his grasp was relentless. "I just want to get away from *you*," she sobbed. "Let me go, you're hurting me."

"Perhaps it's time you felt some pain, Natalie. You prefer to inflict it, don't you, on some poor wretch of a man, raising his hopes to the highest pitch, then dashing them to the ground?"

She uttered a false laugh that held a hysterical note. "You dare to criticize me, when you're notorious for having affairs with any number of women, dropping them and picking up with them again just as it pleases you. You seem *proud* of the fact. You even seem to relish being the subject for a cheap gossip columnist."

"I always play fair, Natalie, that's the difference between us. I never give a woman expectations that I'm not prepared to fulfill. My relationships are straight down the line, honest from the start."

"You make yourself sound positively noble." She sneered. "Well, here's one woman who's escaped from your trap. I despise you, Grant Kilmartin, I loathe and despise you utterly. Is that plain enough for you?"

His eyes molten, Grant drew in a deep, ragged breath, and Natalie quailed at the retort she feared was coming. Then, with a sudden jerk he pulled her against the hard, solid wall of his chest. Before she could react in protest, his lips descended on hers in a bruising, demanding kiss. Instantly, while her mind still fought against him, her treacherous body was ignited with leaping sparks of desire. Grant held her locked hard to his lean frame, his hands roaming over her flesh, kneading its softness. Helplessly she let her own hands slide up across his muscled shoulders and twine around his neck, drawing herself even closer. The blood thundered in her ears, and she felt the heavy thudding of

Grant's heartbeat and heard his rapid, shallow breathing. All awareness of their surroundings vanished and it was just the two of them in some private limbo where nothing but the satisfaction of the senses had any relevance. As she felt the quivering rasp of Grant's tongue exploring her mouth, her fingers curled into the crispness of his dark hair, and she exulted in the insistent throb of his passion.

"I hate to break up such a touching little scene," a female voice drawled nastily from behind Grant. With a jolt he released Natalie and spun around. Petra was standing in the conservatory doorway, her negligent attitude not concealing the look of utter fury in her green eyes. "Sir Matthew has been asking for you, Grant. Something to do with a little presentation from various local residents in gratitude for the shopping arcade. You'd better not keep Mr. Moneybags waiting, had you?"

Grant had already regained his composure. "Okay," he said easily. "I'm coming."

Petra stood aside to let him pass, remarking, "You go ahead. I want a little word with Mrs. Kent first."

Hesitating, Grant glanced at Natalie with questioning eyes. Still weak from the sudden uprush of emotion caused by Grant's kiss, Natalie would dearly have liked to slink away and find someplace to hide. But she was darned if she'd give Petra an easy victory by seeming afraid to face her.

"Didn't you hear what Petra said?" she threw at Grant. "You'd better hurry."

For a splinter of a moment she saw his look of puzzlement; then he made his face a blank mask. With a shrug of his broad shoulders, he departed. Natalie, her knees weak and trembling, leaned against the curving lip of a large stone urn in an effort to appear coolly at ease.

"I suppose you realize," Petra said spitefully, "how

totally unimportant you are to Grant. It amounts to this: his ego needs to be constantly fed with new conquests. The women concerned mean nothing to him."

Natalie crushed down her pain and inquired sarcastically, "But you *do* mean something to him?"

Petra treated her to a superior smile. "The point is, my dear Natalie, that while a little nobody like you might be good enough for Grant to take to bed a couple of times, you'd be quite unsuitable as someone he wants to be coupled with in other people's eyes. A man like Grant, who is going places, needs a woman with good social standing at his side on occasions like this afternoon, to create the image he wants to put across. It's a matter of class, you see."

"It sounds to me," said Natalie, in an attempt to needle her, "as if you're wishing yourself into the role of the second Mrs. Grant Kilmartin."

Petra shrugged. "It wouldn't be such a bad idea, at that. I might give it a thought."

Sick at heart, Natalie turned away. "This seems a rather pointless conversation. I can't imagine why you were so keen to talk to me."

"I merely wanted to do you a good turn, that's all. I thought you might as well realize the hopeless odds against you where Grant is concerned. You're simply not a candidate. So I'd forget about him if you don't want to be hurt."

Natalie forced a smile, trying to stop her lower lip from trembling. "You're wasting your breath. Grant Kilmartin is only of the smallest interest to me."

Petra's beautiful face twisted into an ugly expression. "Is that why you were kissing him so passionately just now? You little fool, can't you see that he was just amusing himself?"

Natalie took a deep, slow breath, determined to gain victory over this sneering woman. "And can't *you* see,

Petra, that I was just amusing myself, too? Why shouldn't I? Grant's a very attractive man. But he's not, as he seems to imagine, God's gift to women. As far as I'm concerned, if you want him, you're welcome to him.''

With her chin in the air, she strode out past the staring Petra. Her heady sense of triumph lasted until she reached the drawing room, where the Astons' tea party was still in full swing. Then suddenly she felt completely drained and exhausted.

Chapter Eleven

$\mathcal{L}$uckily Diane had already said that she and Jeremy were going on somewhere together, so she didn't need a ride home. Seeking out Dudley, who was hovering in a group of people gathered around Sir Matthew, Natalie told him that she was ready to leave. Expecting him to agree at once, she was astonished when he said that he *wasn't*.

"Listen," he said impatiently when she persisted, "I'm twisting the old boy's arm for a slice of the action in one of his offshoot companies. If I can just get him on his own for another ten minutes, that should wrap it up. Then I'll take you home, my sweet."

Natalie felt too upset to press him for details. Instead, she found a quiet corner to wait, where she could hug her misery to herself. Once she accidentally met Grant's eyes across the room, and he gave her a swift, questioning look. Ostentatiously she turned away from him.

When at long last she and Dudley arrived back at Chandler's Wharf, she told him not to come in, saying that she felt too tired for company this evening.

"Tell you what, then, darling," he said brightly, "we'll just relax quietly together for a while. Watch TV and have a drink. Then later on we'll go out for dinner."

"No, I mean it," Natalie insisted. "I don't want you

to come in this time." About to get out of the car, she paused. There was something she ought to have out with him. "Dudley, what did you mean about twisting Sir Matthew's arm?"

"Oh . . . nothing. Just a figure of speech."

"I hope you weren't trading on the fact that I have a connection with the Astons," she said worriedly. "I'd hate them to get the wrong idea."

He dropped her a wink. "Don't get in a panic, darling. I'm playing it cannily. But it's marvelous the way a personal introduction can open doors."

Natalie still felt uneasy, but she didn't have the energy to argue with him right now. When Dudley tried to make plans for tomorrow, she shook her head. She felt impelled suddenly to make it crystal clear to him that there could be no future for them together.

"I don't think it's a good idea for us to see each other anymore," she said. "I mean, there isn't really any point. It's not going to lead us anywhere."

Dudley was horrified. "You can't mean this, darling," he protested. "I thought that everything was going just dandy between us. In fact, I thought you were almost ready to name the day."

"I'm sorry if I've given you that impression, Dudley, but you're quite mistaken. No way am I going to marry you again."

Dudley was silent, his fingers toying restlessly with the ignition key. Then he said slowly, "It's not only me you've given that impression to, my sweet. The Astons are taking it for granted that you and I are tying the knot again."

Natalie sighed impatiently. "That's just because Celia scents romance every time a man and woman are together for five minutes. And you made things worse," she added, "talking to her the way you did."

"I only told her what I feel," he protested. "She and

I had a nice little chat together, and I can tell you this—her ladyship isn't going to like it one bit if things don't work out for us."

She stared at him. "Is that some kind of a threat, Dudley?"

"Don't be silly, darling," he returned, smiling easily. "I'm merely explaining how things stand. There's no reason to be cautious of something just because it happens to suit both your inclinations and your pocket. On the contrary, that makes it doubly worthwhile."

"I . . . I don't follow you," she said, puzzled.

"Then let me spell it out, my sweet. You and I have everything going for us. The old magic is still there, you can't deny it—you said yourself that there's been no one else for you since we split up, except for that one mistake with Kilmartin. So it would work for us, no question. And as for the rest . . . well, we'd have Sir Matthew and Lady Aston smiling on us, and when top people like that smile, a lot of other people jerk into line. You can take it from me that Mr. and Mrs. Dudley Kent would be heading for the big time, you in your designing business, and me in . . . well, whatever comes along, which will be plenty, that's for sure."

A cold feeling clawed up Natalie's spine. "I begin to understand now, Dudley. Your keenness for us to be married again dates from the very moment you discovered that I was doing well—with a big development project in the offing, which would really establish me." She sighed. "I should have realized . . . I should have read the signs."

"Darling, you've got it all wrong," he objected.

"Have I? Then tell me this. Suppose you'd discovered, that day we met in the street, that I had just an ordinary sort of job working in an office. Would you have pursued me then? No, it would have been just a cup of coffee together and then good-bye, wouldn't it?"

He laughed uneasily. "It's a question that doesn't arise."

"It does with me, Dudley, and I know the answer." She clenched her hands together in her lap, sick that she'd let herself be used like this. "I only hope," she went on unhappily, "that you haven't already done too much damage with Sir Matthew and Lady Aston. But I'm going to make sure they understand that there's absolutely no prospect of you and me getting married again."

"Celia won't like it, you know. As a matter of fact—I was saving it up to tell you this evening—she offered us the use of their villa in the south of France for our honeymoon. So you'd better think again, my sweet, if you want to stay in her good books." Dudley was still smiling, confident of his ability to pressure her. Natalie felt a sudden uprush of bitter anger, because now he was expecting to cash in financially from having her as his wife.

She wanted him gone. She wanted never to set eyes on him again. She wanted to be left alone with her wretchedness and misery. With a decisive movement she reached for the door handle. "This is where we say good-bye, Dudley."

"Darling, you haven't been listening," he said sharply. "With me, the world will be your oyster, but without me things could be dodgy for you—especially since you've made an enemy of that Kilmartin chap. I just don't see why you're acting like this."

"But then, you aren't sitting where I'm sitting," she retorted hotly. She didn't want a slanging match with Dudley, though. Her one aim at this moment was to reach the sanctuary of her studio. Taking a juddery breath, she said emphatically, "I'll tell you just once more, Dudley, and that will be it. You and I are through, finished, all washed up. When we met the other day, I should have kept it to just hello and good-bye. I was a fool to see you again, I realize that now, a fool to imagine that we might be friends. If you honestly believe that I've encouraged you to expect more, then I'm truly sorry. But please understand—I shall never, ever agree to marry you again, not in a million years."

Dudley wouldn't accept that. "Listen," he said persuasively, "we've learned our lesson from the mistakes of the past—we're older and wiser now. It could work out just fine, if you'd only give it a chance."

"No, you listen to me," she said firmly. "I'm not arguing with you, Dudley, I'm stating my position. This is the end of the road for us. I want you to get out of my life and stay out. Got that?"

For a few seconds it looked as if he were going to keep up the pressure. Then he gave a negligent shrug. "You're as dumb and gauche as you always were, Natalie. You'll never hit the big time on your own. I'm warning you, you haven't got what it takes. But that's your funeral."

Natalie hesitated a moment longer. Did they really have to part on such a note of hostility? But if that was the price she had to pay to be rid of Dudley, then she'd pay it. With a poor effort at dignity, she opened the car door and got out.

"Good-bye, Dudley," she said in a flat tone. "I don't bear you any ill will, but I've no wish to see you again, ever."

"And good-bye to you!" he snarled. He had driven off before she reached her front door.

Natalie was roused from a state of lethargy by the insistent shrilling of the phone. With a sigh she picked it up and mumbled a resentful hello.

"Natalie, is that you? Celia Aston here."

She gave herself a little shake, wondering what this call portended. Celia sounded agitated. "Is something wrong, Lady Aston?"

"Yes, it's Jodi," she said, and there was a crack in her voice. "She's gone."

"Gone? How do you mean?"

"She stalked out of the apartment just a few minutes ago, and . . . and said she was never coming back."

"Oh, dear!" said Natalie with a sinking heart. Tentatively she asked, "What brought it about, Lady Aston?"

Celia gave a heavy sigh. "Jodi turned up here this afternoon toward the end of our tea party . . . I believe you'd already left by then, Natalie. She looked terribly scruffy, and when her father told her to go and make herself presentable, she was quite appallingly rude to him. Afterward, when we were alone, Matthew laid down the law. He said he simply wasn't going to tolerate his daughter making a spectacle of herself and shaming him in company. They had a dreadful quarrel and Jodi swore at him, using the most unspeakable language. Matthew had to leave right after that, to fly to Edinburgh for a conference first thing in the morning. I was glad, really, thinking that his absence would allow things to cool down. But soon after he'd gone, Jodi came out of her room with a suitcase packed and just walked out. She . . . she said that if her father thought her life-style was so terrible, people might like to know some of the noble things he'd done to get where he is today."

"What did she mean by that?" Natalie queried. "Have you any idea?"

"Not really. But I'm so afraid, Natalie dear, that she might be going to do something very foolish. I . . . I feel frantic with worry, all on my own here. I just had to talk to someone, and you are the only person, dear, that I could possibly confide in. You've always been so sympathetic and understanding about Jodi."

This was just about the worst possible moment to receive a cry for help, Natalie thought ruefully, when her own spirits were at their very lowest ebb. But Celia had been unfailingly kind to her, so she had to make an effort. "Would you like me to come round, Lady Aston?"

"Oh, my dear . . . I couldn't really expect that of you." But the longing in Celia's voice was only too evident.

"I'll come," said Natalie decidedly. "I'll be with you as soon as I can."

Replacing the phone, she was struck by a dismaying thought. Maybe she could guess where Jodi was at this moment. What more likely than for a bewildered young girl to go running to the older man with whom she'd just become infatuated? And if that was what Jodi *had* done, would Grant appreciate that it was a potentially explosive situation which could earn him—whether deservedly or not—the full weight of Sir Matthew Aston's wrath and future enmity? Hating the idea of contacting Grant, she knew she had to warn him.

Grant had a service flat near Sloane Square, and she quickly found his number in the book. Her voice seemed to freeze up when he answered, and it was an effort to get the words out. "Grant . . . this is Natalie."

"Really?" he said in a withering tone. "To what do I owe this pleasure?"

"Listen, it's serious. Is . . . is Jodi Aston with you?"

"What the devil . . . ?" He sounded furiously angry as he went on, "Whether she is or whether she isn't, I fail to see that it's any business of yours."

"Her mother is desperately worried," Natalie explained. "Apparently Jodi walked out after a blazing row with her father. Sir Matthew doesn't know yet, though, but when he does, there'll be all hell to pay. I thought that possibly—"

"You thought wrong, then," Grant retorted sharply. "Even if I felt attracted to a child of that age, I wouldn't be such a damn fool as to get involved."

"I'm sorry," she mumbled, feeling ashamed. But at the same time she felt a sense of elation. "It was just . . . well, because I'd seen Jodi with you at Princess Dock . . ." she stammered by way of explanation.

"The kid was interested—genuinely interested—in the development there. It seems I'd impressed her more than somewhat with what I said at Hartwell Manor. But I'm not such a dimwit that I didn't also realize that Jodi was weaving teenage dreams around me. She's pestered me several times since, dropping in at the office and so forth. This afternoon, when she turned up during her parents' tea party, I decided it was time to call a halt. I did it fairly gently, but she can have been left in no doubt regarding the way I feel about her . . . or rather, *don't* feel."

"That could be what sparked off the row with her father," Natalie said thoughtfully. "If she was in a foul mood over you, Grant, it could account for why she was so rude to him."

"Are you laying the blame for Jodi's disappearance on me?" Grant challenged.

"No, not really. I mean, how could you have guessed she'd do something like this?"

"This is new," he clipped. "Natalie Kent actually having a word to say in my favor."

"Oh, cut that out, Grant. I'd never have called you if I hadn't—"

"If you hadn't jumped to the conclusion that I was busy seducing a babe in arms. You must have a low opinion of my intelligence to think that."

"But before . . . when I said about you and Jodi, that day in your office, you didn't deny it."

"Why the hell should I have denied it? I'm not answerable to you for my actions."

Natalie took a long slow breath. "Grant, I didn't call you to start another fight. I'm glad she's not with you, because it would have been dynamite. But now . . . well, her mother is really frantic with worry about her, and the way it sounded, Jodi might be about to do something stupid."

"Like what?"

"Well, when she slammed out of the apartment, she said something to her mother about exposing some of the things her father had done to get where he is today. Not that I imagine there can be anything much to expose," she added. "I mean, Sir Matthew strikes me as an honest, straightforward sort of businessman."

"Which I've no doubt he is," agreed Grant. "But every inhabitant of this earth, Natalie, has a few secrets he'd prefer not to have shouted abroad. And it doesn't take a lot of effort to blow up small indiscretions into full-scale scandals. One of the penalties of being in the public eye is that other people delight in seeing mud slung—especially if the slinging is done by the man's own family. My guess is that Jodi could end up doing her father a lot of damage if she's really bent on hurting him."

"Oh, Grant, how can we stop her?"

"I think I may know where she is. Listen, I'll pick you up in fifteen minutes, and we'll go there together."

"Where?"

"I'll explain when I see you," he said, and hung up.

Natalie immediately called Lady Aston to tell her that she'd be a bit delayed. "Try not to worry," she urged. "I'm sure everything will turn out okay." She truly believed this, Natalie realized, and wondered why she felt so irrationally confident that Grant would be able to straighten things out.

Getting into the car beside Grant, she was swept by

the familar, breathless sense of panic at his nearness. She had to keep a firm clasp on her emotions and try to concentrate on the *reason* for the two of them being together.

"I have a hunch," he said as they drove off, "that Jodi has gone scampering off to Ashley Baxter. They were talking together this afternoon, and I noticed him giving her one of his business cards. He lives at Primrose Hill. So if Jodi was thinking in terms of hurting her father, she'd know where to go to find an eager listener to any disclosures about him—true or not—that she cares to make."

Primrose Hill wasn't far, and they were there in minutes. Ashley Baxter had the second-floor apartment of a large Regency terrace house. He answered their ring and stood back in exaggerated surprise. "Well, well, visitors. I'm honored."

"Is Jodi Aston with you?" Grant demanded without preamble.

The other man's eyes narrowed. "What makes you think she might be?"

"I asked you a question," Grant said brusquely, "and I want an answer."

A calculating pause; then Ashley Baxter shrugged his elegant shoulders. "She *is* here, as a matter of fact. Quite safe and sound, I assure you. I found her sitting on my doorstep when I arrived home half an hour ago."

"This is where she leaves," said Grant belligerently, and stepped in through the doorway.

"Hold on, friend," said Ashley. "What right have you to—?"

"I don't give a damn about rights," Grant snapped. "Come on, Natalie."

They found Jodi in Ashley's big living room, sitting on a white leather sofa with her legs tucked up, a drink in her hand. There was a scared look in her eyes when she saw them.

"You're coming with us, Jodi," said Grant.

Natalie watched the girl's inner conflict of fear and defiance. Hastily she sat down on the sofa beside Jodi and said gently, "You can't truly want to harm your father, not deep down, just because you and he had a quarrel this afternoon. Please be sensible and let Grant and me take you home."

Jodi's defiance crumbled and she looked utterly wretched. "What's the use of going home after what I said to Mother?" she muttered sullenly.

"Your mother will welcome you with open arms," Natalie assured her. "And she always will, Jodi, no matter how badly you behave. Your father is away tonight, so I don't think he need find out about this episode."

Jodi hesitated, trying to save her pride. But Natalie guessed that she'd already been regretting her impulsive action even before their arrival.

Grant said to Ashley in a tone of heavy threat, "I don't know what stories she's cooked up for you about her father, but just get this into your skull. If you print one derogatory word about Sir Matthew Aston, you won't know what's hit you. Being booted out of Fleet Street will only be the start."

"Empty threats." Ashley sneered. "What could *you* do?"

"Try me, and you'll find out."

Ashley looked uncertain; then he gave in with a careless gesture. "There's nothing worth printing, anyhow. Tame stuff. To be candid, I'll be thankful for you to take the kid off my hands."

Jodi needed no persuading after that. When the three of them were in the car heading for the Astons' apartment, Natalie asked Grant to stop off somewhere for a cup of coffee. "I think it might be a good idea for us to talk things over with Jodi before we take her home," she explained. Two minutes later he pulled up at a small café, and they found a quiet booth at the back.

"First of all," Natalie began, "I do understand your point of view, Jodi, and I sympathize—honestly. Only I want you to ask yourself this: are you making an effort to understand your parents? Okay, so they expect too much of you, I've seen that for myself. But try to imagine the grief it must have been for them to lose their only son—the son in whom your father had pinned such hopes."

Jodi lowered her head and mumbled resentfully, "Do they think I didn't love Keith too? I lost my only brother."

"Yes, I know, Jodi. Your mother once told me how much he meant to you. But I guess this is a case where *you've* got to be the strongest one, because . . . well, you're young, and your life is still ahead of you. For you there's still the chance of making your dreams come true; but for them, the dreams have been smashed. From what I've seen of the situation as an outsider, it looks as if your father is trying to make you into a sort of substitute for the son he lost—right?"

"And how!" Jodi said bitterly. "I'm just his daughter, so I didn't count for anything before. But now that Keith's dead, I'm expected to step into his shoes."

Natalie nodded sympathetically. "You're right, Jodi, it's grossly unfair that men should put such high value on having a son. But that's the way it's been all down the ages, and the situation isn't going to change overnight just because women are beginning to win the battle for sex equality. It's something that has to be accepted." She took a deep breath and continued, "What you *don't* have to accept, though, is your father trying to mold you into someone you aren't. You've every right to resist him, Jodi. But not by being sulky and quarrelsome and generally awkward. It would be much better to face up to your father and tell him pleasantly but firmly what it is that you want to make of your life."

"He wouldn't listen."

"Not at first, maybe. You'd have to be patient and keep trying. But he'd come round in the end, because basically he's a fair-minded man, and he'd respect you for being determined. You know that in your heart, don't you?"

Jodi nodded jerkily. She still looked bowed down by misery, but Natalie thought she could detect a spark of hope in the girl.

"Do you know yet what it is you really want to do, Jodi?" she probed gently.

There was silence. Then suddenly it all came pouring out in a rush. "Well, there's this organization for giving aid to third-world countries. If you're chosen, they give you a six-month training course and then you get sent abroad for three years. You can do all sorts of things like teaching hygiene and helping to dig wells and giving out food where there's been a famine—really important work. When I mentioned it at home once, saying I knew someone who'd done it and it sounded very interesting, Daddy wanted to know how much salary they paid. As if money mattered," she finished scornfully.

As they got up to leave, Natalie said, "I'd like to call your mother to say we're bringing you home now. She's been so worried, and it'll be such a relief to her. When we get there we'll just drop you off and leave you to explain things. You might want to edit the truth a little bit . . . that's up to you. But remember this, Jodi, she really does care about you and she's anxious for you to be happy. So why not talk to her about what you want to do with your life. Treat her as an ally instead of as your enemy, and you'll find it a great help having her on your side."

On the phone, Celia was overjoyed and plied Natalie with questions. But she parried them firmly. "Let Jodi tell you herself, Lady Aston, in her own way."

"Whatever you say, Natalie, dear. I'm so thankful to you for what you've done."

"I was only too glad to help," she said lightly, echoing the words Celia had previously used to her.

"A real Miss Fixit, aren't you?" Grant said ironically as they watched Jodi disappear into the entrance of the mansion block where the Astons lived.

Natalie turned on him with a flare of anger. "Listen, I'm grateful for your help over Jodi, but I can do without your sneering comments." A cruising taxi came into view, and impulsively Natalie put her hand out of the car window to flag it down. But as the driver slowed, Grant impatiently signaled him to keep going.

"Don't want me, then?" The driver leaned out of his cab. "Is that all right by you, miss?"

"I suppose so," she said reluctantly, and the taxi sped away.

Grant made no move to start the car, and the silence stretched between them. Then, as he seemed about to say something, Natalie snapped, "Since you're so keen to drive me home, then kindly get on with it."

"Very well," he said coldly.

Neither of them spoke on the short trip back to Chandler's Wharf, and the tension mounted to screaming pitch. As soon as Grant turned into the courtyard and parked, Natalie mumbled good night and jumped out quickly. But Grant caught up with her at her front door.

"No, you're not going to duck out on me like that," he grated. "We've got to have a talk, Natalie."

"There's nothing to talk about," she said tersely. "You're not coming in."

"Oh yes I am! And I'm staying until we've got things straightened out between us."

"If you must, then," she said with an elaborate shrug of resignation. But inwardly her heart was thudding against her ribs and little tingles of excitement raced along her veins. "Well?" she demanded as Grant closed the door behind them.

"Watching you tonight handling that mixed-up Aston kid," he began hesitantly, "something got through to me that I'd been shutting my eyes to, because it didn't accord with the Grant Kilmartin philosophy of life."

"Which is?" she asked in a shaky voice.

"That involves a long story."

"Make it short," she advised.

He gave her a curious, self-effacing kind of smile that sent her pulses leaping even higher. "Why should I make it short? Haven't we got all the time in the world? Natalie, for goodness' sake give me a chance. Sit down and let me talk to you."

After a moment's hesitation she sat down with him on the sofa, but she kept a safe distance between them. "Right. Start talking."

"You're not making it easy for me, are you?" he said reproachfully, then gave a wry smile. "Okay, why should you? I haven't exactly made things easy for you." Natalie didn't comment, and after a brief pause he went on, "You know the quote about no man being an island? Well, I reckoned that I *was,* girt around by unscalable cliffs and lots of ocean. Grant Kilmartin was the whole works, complete and self-contained. I *used* other people, I didn't *need* them."

"And . . . and you see things differently now?" she queried in a husky whisper.

"I'm learning to, Natalie, and I have a very good teacher. Tonight helped to confirm what I'd already realized—that you care about other people, about their feelings. This business with Jodi . . . you didn't need to get involved. You could have just shrugged your shoulders and left her and the Astons to get on with it."

"I'd have expected you," she said in remembered bitterness, before she could stop herself, "to see my motive as trying to dig in better with the Astons."

"The thought never once crossed my mind, Natalie. And that's significant, don't you agree?" Grant got to his feet, as if he could no longer contain himself sitting down. "Let me go back in time, to help you understand. I took what is sneeringly thought of as the classic, surefire road to success: I married the boss's daughter. Only I never saw it like that. I worked for Melissa's father as a construction supervisor in his development company. I was ambitious, and the future looked rosy. It was in those days that I handled this Chandler's Wharf conversion. Then I met Melissa at a Christmas party and fell in love with her instantly. It was the real thing, so I honestly believed. We were married a few months later, and I regarded the pay rise I received as no more than my due. It was some while before it finally got through to me what my new role was—a highly paid playboy husband for Melissa, with no job responsibilities to spoil the fun. I kept trying to do a real job, but my father-in-law didn't want that. Finally, when I was getting desperate, I was given a seat on the board of directors. Thankfully, I saw this as a chance to flex my muscles and take some real responsibility in the firm. That way, I thought, our marriage could be saved . . . because I was still in love with Melissa, despite everything. The end came soon afterward, when my wife announced that she wanted us to go off on a luxurious round-the-world cruise. I told her it was impossible for me to be away from work for so long, and she laughed in my face. From her I learned, and she didn't mince her words, that the directorship was nothing more than a fancy title given me at her instigation. We had a final blazing row and I walked out. Next morning I quit my job. As soon as the divorce was through, Melissa married again. This time she chose someone more amenable . . . a former race-car driver, who is still dazed by his good luck, I gather, in being the nominal head of the South African branch of her father's organization.''

"And having quit your job," Natalie prompted, "you set up the Kilmartin Development Corporation?"

"Right. I was determined to show Melissa—and the rest of the world—that I could make it big on my own. I worked flat out, all the hours there were, and I sweet-talked my way into getting the financial backing I needed to carry me through. I'd just about reached the stage of making my mark on the construction scene, with my first really big project lined up, when you walked into my life. You talked about how you could help me—and help was something I did not want. I tried to throw you out, Natalie, and yet I couldn't . . . there was something about you that got to me. I argued to myself that what I felt was merely a sex thing like all the others. So I played along with you, only to find myself getting deeper and deeper involved." He pulled a wry face at her. "Can you understand now why it was I went up the wall when you came to the rescue over the Princess Dock scheme? I couldn't bear the thought that you'd made me beholden to you.''

"I didn't think of it that way, Grant," she protested faintly.

"How was I to know, when I was busy seeing self-interest as your only possible motive? But you finally swept away the barricades I'd erected around myself, and forced me to face the truth.''

"The . . . the truth?" she faltered.

He put out a hand, touching the sheening silk of her

hair, and Natalie trembled at his touch. "The fact, sweet, adorable Natalie, that I'd fallen in love with you."

She made a little inarticulate sound from the sudden tightness of her throat—a sob of relief, of joy, a plea that Grant wasn't, even now, playing with her. But that last thought she thrust away as unthinkable.

Grant dropped to his knees and cupped her face between his two hands, the thumbs caressing her jawline. "Do you think it's possible, darling Natalie, that you might someday come to love me in return?"

"Come to love you!" she echoed brokenly. "Oh . . . you fool, you adorable idiot, Grant, I *do* love you . . . I've loved you ever since that night we . . . Before that . . . from before I even knew that I loved you. . . ."

His arms slid around her slender body, and the descent of his lips on hers smothered any further outpouring of her heart. They clung together for long, throbbing moments, locked not in passion but in the joy of thankfulness. At long last Grant drew back enough to look tenderly into her eyes while his fingers twined into the scented softness of her hair.

"I warn you," he said huskily, "I shall be terribly possessive and ferociously jealous."

"You'll have nothing to be jealous about," she whispered.

"Dudley?"

Natalie shook her head emphatically. "Seeing him the way I've been doing was all because of you, Grant. To get back at you. Even so, I still don't owe Dudley anything. This afternoon I told him that I don't want to see him ever again." She drew in a tremulous breath, afraid of the question, but needing his honest answer. "Grant . . . how about you? I could never accept it if I thought you'd ever want to . . ."

His dark eyes held tender reproach. "You can't imagine that I'd ever look at another woman, darling."

She voiced just a name, as he had done. "Petra?"

"Like you with Dudley, I used Petra as a weapon against you. But Petra won't suffer more than a small dent in her pride. She's always been a good-time girl, ready to tag along with whichever man best suited her mood. I've never cheated or misled her in any way. I want you to believe, darling, that ever since . . . ever since the day you first came walking into my office, there's been no one else for me. Not Petra, not anyone. You captured my heart that day, and I've been your prisoner ever since."

They kissed again, lingeringly, and this time the passion flared. In Natalie's heart there was a wonderful blend of calm and excitement—the sort of calm that comes from arriving home after a long and dangerous journey, plus the heady excitement of being held close in a lover's arms. Between kisses they murmured softly to one another, broken phrases of love and tenderness, of soaring desire. Grant's hands slid over her body in a fever of possession, as if to reassure himself that she really and truly was his to make love to. And Natalie exulted in the knowledge that he was her man, that he loved her, that he wanted and needed her.

Suddenly there was a swift-surging urgency to their passion which rushed them to a pitch of longing too intense to permit a moment's delay. They sank down onto the fleecy softness of the carpet, each hungrily dragging off the other's garments until they lay naked together. Their bodies joined, and in a quick crescendo of need they made love again as rapturously as that first time, till all heaven erupted in a glittering cascade of falling stars.

In the golden haze of afterward, Grant touched his lips to hers in a hundred tiny kisses. "Let me carry you off to bed, Mrs. Kilmartin . . . as you are my wife, Natalie, darling, in every way except for a little piece of paper—which we'll see about tomorrow. But tonight . . ."

"Yes, please, Grant." She nodded in a blissful daze of contentment.

In her wide bed they lay close with their limbs entwined, and Natalie gloried in the knowledge that, from now on, this would be the pattern of their nights. With his fingertips tracing lazy, sensuous circles around her breasts and across the firm softness of her stomach, they talked of the future, making plans.

"Partners, darling, that's what we'll be," he murmured, kissing the velvet-soft lobe of her ear. "No more wanting to do it all on my own."

"Partners," she whispered with a happy sigh. "Yes, I like the thought of that."

"What a team we'll make," he enthused. "You and me together."

She laughed. "Oh, I do love you, Grant."

"And I, my darling, adore every particle of you. I worship you, and I find you infinitely desirable."

She smiled at him impishly. "When you've told me that a thousand times, I just might start believing you."

"Remember what I said to you before about actions speaking louder than words?" There was a throaty, meaningful chuckle in his voice.

"What's that supposed to mean?" she asked, shamelessly leading him on.

"Things like this . . . and this." He pressed his lips to hers, his tongue erotically probing her mouth while the hand on her breast teased the nipple to a tingling ecstasy of desire.

"I hope it's going to be a long lesson," she gurgled when they broke off to draw breath.

"As long as it takes to convince you, darling."

"In that case," she tossed back brazenly as she let her hands roam across his muscled contours in a journey of sweet exploration, "I'd better warn you that I'm a very slow learner. It's likely to take you forever."

"Make it forever-plus-plus," he said, pulling her closer against his hard body, "and you've got yourself a deal."

If you enjoyed
this book...

...you will enjoy a Special Edition Book Club membership even more.

It will bring you each new title, as soon as it is published every month, delivered right to your door.

15-Day Free Trial Offer

We will send you 6 new Silhouette Special Editions to keep for 15 days absolutely free! If you decide not to keep them, send them back to us, you pay nothing. But if you enjoy them as much as we think you will, keep them and pay the invoice enclosed with your trial shipment. You will then automatically become a member of the Special Edition Book Club and receive 6 more romances every month. There is no minimum number of books to buy and you can cancel at any time.

▬ ▬ ▬ ▬ FREE CHARTER MEMBERSHIP COUPON ▬ ▬ ▬ ▬

 Silhouette Special Editions, Dept. SESE7R
120 Brighton Road, Clifton, NJ 07012

Please send me 6 Silhouette Special Editions to keep for 15 days, absolutely free. I understand I am not obligated to join the Silhouette Special Editions Book Club unless I decide to keep them.

Name _____

Address _____

City _____

State _____ Zip _____

This offer expires March 31, 1984

Silhouette Special Edition

MORE ROMANCE FOR
A SPECIAL WAY TO RELAX
$1.95 each

2 ☐ Hastings	21 ☐ Hastings	41 ☐ Halston	60 ☐ Thorne
3 ☐ Dixon	22 ☐ Howard	42 ☐ Drummond	61 ☐ Beckman
4 ☐ Vitek	23 ☐ Charles	43 ☐ Shaw	62 ☐ Bright
5 ☐ Converse	24 ☐ Dixon	44 ☐ Eden	63 ☐ Wallace
6 ☐ Douglass	25 ☐ Hardy	45 ☐ Charles	64 ☐ Converse
7 ☐ Stanford	26 ☐ Scott	46 ☐ Howard	65 ☐ Cates
8 ☐ Halston	27 ☐ Wisdom	47 ☐ Stephens	66 ☐ Mikels
9 ☐ Baxter	28 ☐ Ripy	48 ☐ Ferrell	67 ☐ Shaw
10 ☐ Thiels	29 ☐ Bergen	49 ☐ Hastings	68 ☐ Sinclair
11 ☐ Thornton	30 ☐ Stephens	50 ☐ Browning	69 ☐ Dalton
12 ☐ Sinclair	31 ☐ Baxter	51 ☐ Trent	70 ☐ Clare
13 ☐ Beckman	32 ☐ Douglass	52 ☐ Sinclair	71 ☐ Skillern
14 ☐ Keene	33 ☐ Palmer	53 ☐ Thomas	72 ☐ Belmont
15 ☐ James	35 ☐ James	54 ☐ Hohl	73 ☐ Taylor
16 ☐ Carr	36 ☐ Dailey	55 ☐ Stanford	74 ☐ Wisdom
17 ☐ John	37 ☐ Stanford	56 ☐ Wallace	75 ☐ John
18 ☐ Hamilton	38 ☐ John	57 ☐ Thornton	76 ☐ Ripy
19 ☐ Shaw	39 ☐ Milan	58 ☐ Douglass	77 ☐ Bergen
20 ☐ Musgrave	40 ☐ Converse	59 ☐ Roberts	78 ☐ Gladstone

Silhouette Special Edition

MORE ROMANCE FOR
A SPECIAL WAY TO RELAX

$2.25 each

79 ☐ Hastings	87 ☐ Dixon	95 ☐ Doyle	103 ☐ Taylor
80 ☐ Douglass	88 ☐ Saxon	96 ☐ Baxter	104 ☐ Wallace
81 ☐ Thornton	89 ☐ Meriwether	97 ☐ Shaw	105 ☐ Sinclair
82 ☐ McKenna	90 ☐ Justin	98 ☐ Hurley	106 ☐ John
83 ☐ Major	91 ☐ Stanford	99 ☐ Dixon	107 ☐ Ross
84 ☐ Stephens	92 ☐ Hamilton	100 ☐ Roberts	108 ☐ Stephens
85 ☐ Beckman	93 ☐ Lacey	101 ☐ Bergen	
86 ☐ Halston	94 ☐ Barrie	102 ☐ Wallace	

**LOOK FOR SUMMER COURSE IN LOVE
BY CAROLE HALSTON AVAILABLE IN SEPTEMBER**

**AND A THISTLE IN THE SPRING BY LINDA SHAW
IN OCTOBER.**

SILHOUETTE SPECIAL EDITION, Department SE/2
1230 Avenue of the Americas
New York, NY 10020

Please send me the books I have checked above. I am enclosing $_____
(please add 50¢ to cover postage and handling. NYS and NYC residents
please add appropriate sales tax). Send check or money order—no cash or
C.O.D.'s please. Allow six weeks for delivery.

NAME _____

ADDRESS _____

CITY _____ STATE/ZIP _____

Love, passion and adventure will be yours FREE for 15 days... with Tapestry™ historical romances!

"Long before women could read and write, tapestries were used to record events and stories . . . especially the exploits of courageous knights and their ladies."

And now there's a new kind of tapestry...

In the pages of Tapestry™ romance novels, you'll find love, intrigue, and historical touches that really make the stories come alive!

You'll meet brave Guyon d'Arcy, a Norman knight . . . handsome Comte Andre de Crillon, a Huguenot royalist . . . rugged Branch Taggart, a feuding American rancher . . . and more. And on each journey back in time, you'll experience tender romance and searing passion . . . and learn about the way people lived and loved in earlier times than ours.

We think you'll be so delighted with Tapestry romances, you won't want to miss a single one! We'd like to send you 2 books each month, as soon as they are published, through our Tapestry Home Subscription Service.℠ Look them over for 15 days, free. If not delighted, simply return them and owe nothing. But if you enjoy them as much as we think you will, pay the invoice enclosed. There's never any additional charge for this convenient service — we pay all postage and handling costs.

To receive your Tapestry historical romances, fill out the coupon below and mail it to us today. You're on your way to all the love, passion, and adventure of times gone by!

HISTORICAL *Tapestry* ROMANCES

Tapestry Home Subscription Service, Dept. TPSE 07
120 Brighton Road, Box 5020, Clifton, NJ 07012

Yes, I'd like to receive 2 exciting Tapestry historical romances each month as soon as they are published. The books are mine to examine for 15 days, free. If not delighted, I can return them and owe nothing. There is never a charge for this convenient home delivery—no postage, handling, or any other hidden charges. If I decide to keep the books, I will pay the invoice enclosed.

I understand there is no minimum number of books I must buy, and that I can cancel this arrangement at any time.

Name		
Address		
City	State	Zip
Signature	(If under 18, parent or guardian must sign.)	

This offer expires March 31, 1984.

Tapestry™ is a trademark of Simon & Schuster.

Silhouette Desire
15-Day Trial Offer
A new romance series
that explores
contemporary relationships
in exciting detail

Six Silhouette Desire romances, free for 15 days!
We'll send you six new Silhouette Desire romances
to look over for 15 days, absolutely free! If you decide
not to keep the books, return them and owe nothing.

Six books a month, free home delivery. If you like
Silhouette Desire romances as much as we think you
will, keep them and return your payment with the
invoice. Then we will send you six new books every
month to preview, just as soon as they are published.
You pay only for the books you decide to keep, and
you never pay postage and handling.

— — — **MAIL TODAY** — — —

Silhouette Desire, Dept. SDSE 7S
120 Brighton Road, Clifton, NJ 07012

Please send me 6 Silhouette Desire romances to keep for
15 days, absolutely free. I understand I am not obligated
to join the Silhouette Desire Book Club unless I decide
to keep them.

Name_____

Address_____

City_____

State_____ Zip_____

This offer expires March 31, 1984

READERS' COMMENTS ON SILHOUETTE SPECIAL EDITIONS:

"I just finished reading the first six Silhouette Special Edition Books and I had to take the opportunity to write you and tell you how much I enjoyed them. I enjoyed all the authors in this series. Best wishes on your Silhouette Special Editions line and many thanks."

—B.H.*, Jackson, OH

"The Special Editions are really special and I enjoyed them very much! I am looking forward to next month's books."

—R.M.W.*, Melbourne, FL

"I've just finished reading four of your first six Special Editions and I enjoyed them very much. I like the more sensual detail and longer stories. I will look forward each month to your new Special Editions."

—L.S.*, Visalia, CA

"Silhouette Special Editions are — 1.) Superb! 2.) Great! 3.) Delicious! 4.) Fantastic! . . . Did I leave anything out? These are books that an adult woman can read . . . I love them!"

—H.C.*, Monterey Park, CA

*names available on request